Network Topology and Fault-Tolerant Consensus

Synthesis Lectures on Distributed Computing Theory

Editor
Michel Raynal, *University of Rennes, France and Hong Kong Polytechnic University*

Founding Editor
Nancy Lynch, *Massachusetts Institute of Technology*

Synthesis Lectures on Distributed Computing Theory was founded by Nancy Lynch of the Massachusetts Institute of Technology, and is now edited by Michel Raynal of the University of Rennes, France and Hong Kong Polytechnic University. The series publishes 50- to 150-page publications on topics pertaining to distributed computing theory. The scope largely follows the purview of premier information and computer science conferences, such as ACM PODC, DISC, SPAA, OPODIS, CONCUR, DialM-POMC, ICDCS, SODA, Sirocco, SSS, and related conferences. Potential topics include, but not are limited to: distributed algorithms and lower bounds, algorithm design methods, formal modeling and verification of distributed algorithms, and concurrent data structures.

Network Topology and Fault-Tolerant Consensus
Dimitris Sakavalas and Lewis Tseng
2019

Introduction to Distributed Self-Stabilizing Algorithms
Karine Altisen, Stéphane Devismes, Swan Dubois, and Franck Petit
2019

Distributed Computing Perls
Gadi Taubenfeld
2018

Decidability of Parameterized Verification
Roderick Bloem, Swen Jacobs, Ayrat Khalimov, Igor Konnov, Sasha Rubin, Helmut Veith, and Josef Widder
2015

Impossibility Results for Distributed Computing
Hagit Attiya and Faith Ellen
2014

Distributed Graph Coloring: Fundamentals and Recent Developments
Leonid Barenboim and Michael Elkin
2013

Distributed Computing by Oblivious Mobile Robots
Paola Flocchini, Giuseppe Prencipe, and Nicola Santoro
2012

Quorum Systems: With Applications to Storage and Consensus
Marko Vukolić
2012

Link Reversal Algorithms
Jennifer L. Welch and Jennifer E. Walter
2011

Cooperative Task-Oriented Computing: Algorithms and Complexity
Chryssis Georgiou and Alexander A. Shvartsman
2011

New Models for Population Protocols
Othon Michail, Ioannis Chatzigiannakis, and Paul G. Spirakis
2011

The Theory of Timed I/O Automata, Second Edition
Dilsun K. Kaynar, Nancy Lynch, Roberto Segala, and Frits Vaandrager
2010

Principles of Transactional Memory
Rachid Guerraoui and Michał Kapałka
2010

Fault-tolerant Agreement in Synchronous Message-passing Systems
Michel Raynal
2010

Communication and Agreement Abstractions for Fault-Tolerant Asynchronous Distributed Systems
Michel Raynal
2010

The Mobile Agent Rendezvous Problem in the Ring
Evangelos Kranakis, Danny Krizanc, and Euripides Markou
2010

Network Topology and Fault-Tolerant

Consensus Dimitris Sakavalas and Lewis Tseng

ISBN: 978-3-031-00886-3   paperback
ISBN: 978-3-031-02014-8   eBook
ISBN: 978-3-031-00132-1   hardcover

DOI 10.1007/978-3-031-02014-8

A Publication in the Springer series
SYNTHESIS LECTURES ON DISTRIBUTED COMPUTING THEORY

Lecture #16
Series Editor: Michel Raynal, *University of Rennes, France and Hong Kong Polytechnic University*
Founding Editor: Nancy Lynch, *Massachusetts Institute of Technology*
Series ISSN
Print 2155-1626   Electronic 2155-1634

Network Topology and Fault-Tolerant Consensus

Dimitris Sakavalas
Boston College

Lewis Tseng
Boston College

SYNTHESIS LECTURES ON DISTRIBUTED COMPUTING THEORY #16

ABSTRACT

As the structure of contemporary communication networks grows more complex, practical networked distributed systems become prone to component failures. Fault-tolerant consensus in message-passing systems allows participants in the system to agree on a common value despite the malfunction or misbehavior of some components. It is a task of fundamental importance for distributed computing, due to its numerous applications.

We summarize studies on the topological conditions that determine the feasibility of consensus, mainly focusing on directed networks and the case of restricted topology knowledge at each participant. Recently, significant efforts have been devoted to fully characterize the underlying communication networks in which variations of fault-tolerant consensus can be achieved. Although the deduction of analogous topological conditions for undirected networks of known topology had shortly followed the introduction of the problem, their extension to the directed network case has been proven a highly non-trivial task. Moreover, global knowledge restrictions, inherent in modern large-scale networks, require more elaborate arguments concerning the locality of distributed computations. In this work, we present the techniques and ideas used to resolve these issues.

Recent studies indicate a number of parameters that affect the topological conditions under which consensus can be achieved, namely, the fault model, the degree of system synchrony (synchronous vs. asynchronous), the type of agreement (exact vs. approximate), the level of topology knowledge, and the algorithm class used (general vs. iterative). We outline the feasibility and impossibility results for various combinations of the above parameters, extensively illustrating the relation between network topology and consensus.

KEYWORDS

consensus, network topology, message-passing systems, asynchronous systems, synchronous systems, topological conditions, broadcast, reliable message transmission, local adversary, general adversary

Contents

List of Figures xi

List of Tables xiii

List of Algorithms xv

Preface xvii

Acknowledgments xxi

PART I   Network Topology and Fault-Tolerance **1**

1   Introduction 3

   1.1   Computational Model 3

       1.1.1 Synchrony 4

       1.1.2 Inputs and Outputs 5

       1.1.3 Initial Knowledge of Processes 5

   1.2   Adversary Model 6

       1.2.1 Corruptible Sets 6

       1.2.2 Corruption Type 7

       1.2.3 Corruption Time 7

   1.3   Consensus Problems 8

       1.3.1 Exact Consensus 8

       1.3.2 Approximate and Asymptotic Consensus 10

   1.4   Algorithm Constraints 11

       1.4.1 Synchronous IAC Algorithms 12

       1.4.2 Asynchronous IAC Algorithms 12

       1.4.3 Comparison of General and Iterative Algorithms 13

   1.5   Summary of Results 14

   1.6   Related Work 15

       1.6.1 Related Problems in Incomplete Networks 15

       1.6.2 Recent Progress 16

2 **Consensus and Network Topology** **19**

    2.1   The Undirected Network Case 19

        2.1.1 Synchronous Networks 20

        2.1.2 Asynchronous Networks 22

    2.2   The Directed Network Case 23

    2.3   Network Preliminaries 26

        2.3.1 The Network 26

        2.3.2 Graph Terminology 26

        2.3.3 Communication Redundancy Between Sets 27

    2.4   Network Topology and Consensus 28

        2.4.1 General Algorithms 28

        2.4.2 Iterative Algorithms 29

    2.5   Relations among Tight Conditions 30

PART II   **Consensus with a Global Adversary** **33**

3 **Synchronous Crash Fault Tolerance** **35**

    3.1   Topological Conditions and Implications 35

    3.2   Necessity of Conditions CCS-I and CCS-G 37

    3.3   Approximate Consensus Algorithm 38

    3.4   Exact Consensus Algorithm 42

        3.4.1 Algorithm Min-Max 42

        3.4.2 Correctness of Algorithm Min-Max 43

4 **Asynchronous Crash Fault Tolerance** **45**

    4.1   Conditions Relations and Implications 45

    4.2   Iterative Approximate Consensus 47

        4.2.1 Necessity of Condition CCA-I 48

        4.2.2 Sufficiency of Condition CCA-I 48

    4.3   General Approximate Consensus 53

        4.3.1 Necessity of Condition CCA-G 53

        4.3.2 Sufficiency of Condition CCA-G 53

5   Byzantine Fault Tolerance **57**

5.1   Implications of Conditions BCS-I and BCS-G 57

5.2   Reduced Graph 59

5.3   Iterative Approximate Consensus 61

    5.3.1   Necessity of Condition BCS-I 61

    5.3.2   Sufficiency of Condition BCS-I 63

    5.3.3   Condition BCA-I 65

5.4   General Algorithms 66

    5.4.1   Necessity of Condition BCS-G 67

    5.4.2   Sufficiency of Condition BCS-G 67

6   Relay Depth and Approximate Consensus **77**

6.1   Iterative k-Hop Algorithm 77

6.2   Asynchronous Crash Fault Tolerance 78

    6.2.1   The $k = 1$ Case 78

    6.2.2   General k Case 79

    6.2.3   Condition Relation 81

    6.2.4   Topology Discovery and Unlimited Relay Depth 82

6.3   Synchronous Byzantine Fault Tolerance 85

    6.3.1   Condition BCS-k 85

    6.3.2   Necessity and Sufficiency 85

PART III   Other Adversarial Models **89**

7   Broadcast Under Local Adversaries **91**

7.1   Preliminaries and Topological Conditions 92

7.2   Necessity of Condition PLC for *ad hoc* Broadcast 94

7.3   Feasibility of *ad hoc* Broadcast 95

7.4   Relation with Consensus Feasibility 97

7.5   Model Extensions 98

    7.5.1   Non-Uniform Model 98

    7.5.2   Directed Networks 98

7.6   Maximum Tolerable Number of Local Faults 99

    7.6.1   Bounds on Max CPA Resilience 100

    7.6.2   Efficient Approximation of Max CPA Resilience 101

8   General Adversary **105**

8.1   Approximate Byzantine Consensus Under a General Adversary 106
    8.1.1   Impossibility of Approximate Consensus 106
    8.1.2   General Adversary IAC Algorithm 107

8.2   Reliable Communication Under Partial Topology Knowledge 109
    8.2.1   Preliminaries 109
    8.2.2   The Algebraic Structure of Partial Knowledge 110
    8.2.3   Necessary Topological Condition 112
    8.2.4   Sufficiency of Condition GRC 113
    8.2.5   Relation with Consensus Feasibility 117

Bibliography **119**

Authors' Biographies **129**

List of Figures

2.1   A weakly connected network where consensus is impossible. 24

2.2   A network that is *not* strongly connected but still allows consensus. 24

2.3   An example network that tolerates one crash fault. 25

2.4   A network that illustrates redundant communication between sets. 27

2.5   Relations of the tight topological conditions. All inclusions are strict. 32

5.1   Illustration for the necessity proof of Theorem 2.14. The case of
$C \cup R \overset{f+1}{\not\twoheadrightarrow} L$ and $L \cup C \overset{f+1}{\not\twoheadrightarrow} R$. 62

7.1   Indistinguishable graphs G and G' in the *ad hoc* model. 94

7.2   A tight example for the approximation ratio. 103

8.1   Example of the joint knowledge operation $\oplus$. 111

List of Tables

1.1   Summary of recent results on directed networks 15

2.1   Tight conditions for undirected networks with a global adversary 20

List of Algorithms

3.1   *Average* 39

3.2   Min-Max 43

3.3   Compute(t, *Function*) 43

4.4   LocWA (Local-Wait-Average) 49

4.5   WA (Wait-and-Average) 55

5.6   IBS (Iterative-Byzantine-Synchronous) 64

5.7   IBA (Iterative-Byzantine-Asynchonous) 66

5.8   BC (Byzantine-Consensus) 70

5.9   Propagate (P, D) 72

5.10   Equality (D) 73

6.11 k-LocWA (Local-Wait-Average) 80

6.12   LWA (Learn-Wait-Average) 84

6.13   Trim($\mathcal{M}_i$) 87

6.14   ISB (Iterative-Synchronous-Byzantine) 88

7.15   CPA (Certified-Propagation-Algorithm) 96

7.16   Existence check of a minimum m-level ordering for (G, s) 102

7.17   2-Approximation of $f_{\max}^{\mathrm{CPA}}$ 102

8.18   G-IAC (General-adversary-IAC) 108

8.19   RMT-PKA (RMT Partial Knowledge Algorithm) 114

8.20   Decision(M_r, *lastmsg*) 115

8.21   Nocover(M) 116

Preface

The rapid growth of networked systems (e.g., the Internet, sensor networks, social networks, financial networks, etc.) naturally presents increased vulnerability concerns regarding their components. Considerations arising from this phenomenon are formally addressed in the study of *fault-tolerant distributed computing*. In this book, we focus mainly on the *fault-tolerant consensus* problem, which allows interacting participants of a networked system to reach an agreement despite the presence of misbehavior. Consensus is a primitive of fundamental importance for distributed computing and cryptographic protocols due to its wide range of applications. For instance, it serves as a building-block for redundant flight control systems, for the assertion of consistency among replicated databases, or for electronic voting and cryptocurrencies.

The *fault-tolerant consensus* problem has received significant attention since the seminal works of Lamport, Shostak, and Pease [50, 78] in 1980. In their setup, each participant is given an input value initially, and after a finite amount of time, each fault-free participant should produce an output value. In this book, we summarize recent results regarding both *exact* and *approximate* consensus in the context of deterministic algorithms and message-passing networks, where the participants communicate via messages. For exact consensus, all fault-free participants eventually agree on and output a common value, which depends on the initial values of all participants. For approximate consensus, the outputs of the participants must eventually be arbitrarily close to each other. Approximate consensus is of particular interest and has been the focus of many recent studies. Apart from its wide applications in the control systems area, its significance for the distributed computing community mainly comes from the fact that it can be used to overcome the impossibility or the high complexity of achieving consensus in certain models.

In general, the feasibility and efficiency of realizing distributed tasks depends on a number of parameters considered in this book and outlined in the following.

Adversary One can easily observe that if the adversary can corrupt any subset of participants and make them misbehave in any way, then the achievement of most meaningful distributed tasks becomes impossible or vague. Therefore, fault-tolerance studies assume different restrictions on the adversary which are determined by the adversary model. Specifically, the model defines the power of the adversary in terms of the misbehavior type and the family of sets that can be corrupted during an execution of the given algorithm.

In this book, we focus on the results addressing *crash* faults (fail-stop faults), where some participants may prematurely stop executing the protocol, and *Byzantine* faults, where some participants may have arbitrary misbehavior, by blocking, rerouting, or even altering a message that they should normally relay intact to specific nodes. Regarding the corruptible sets of participants, we mainly focus on the classic threshold model in which there is a fixed bound on the number of participants that may be corrupted in the system, while we also present feasibility results for the cases of a local and a general adversary which are more recently studied. The former model has applications in systems where participants can only use local information, while the latter encompasses all known adversary models by modeling a situation where arbitrary coalitions of faulty participants are possible.

Timing and System Synchrony   Another parameter that significantly affects the feasibility of distributed tasks is the amount of synchrony between interacting participants. The synchrony notion includes two parameters; namely, the message delivery delay and the relative speeds with which the participants take consecutive computational steps. In order to illustrate these notions, it is common to concentrate on two extreme models: the synchronous model and the asynchronous one.

- In the synchronous case, it is assumed that there are bounds on both message delivery delays and relative speeds of the participants. Without loss of generality, one can assume that all message deliveries are instant and all participants perform computations with the exact same speed.

- In the asynchronous model, no fixed bounds on the delays and relative computation speeds are assumed. Specifically, the delivery delay of messages is finite, but no known time bound is assumed on it, and the computation speeds may arbitrarily differ.

Network   *Network topology* which defines the communication capability between all pairs of participants naturally affects the degree to which certain distributed tasks can be achieved. Moreover, the initial knowledge of the topology possessed by the participants has also proven crucial in the determination of the feasibility condition. Regarding consensus feasibility, tight conditions on the network topology have shortly followed the introduction of the problem for the case of undirected networks where participants have full topology knowledge; these well-known results are outlined in the first two chapters of the book.

We give a more detailed presentation of sufficient and necessary topological conditions in the case of *directed networks* and the case of *restricted topology knowledge*. The study of directed networks is largely motivated by wireless networks, in which the different transmit radii may result in one-way communication between two participants. More importantly, it has been shown that the arguments underlying the topological conditions in undirected networks *cannot* be trivially extended to the directed case; thus, the latter case presents an extra level of difficulty which has been addressed in a series of works summarized in this book. The motivation behind the restricted topology knowledge of participants stems from large-scale networks, in which the estimation of global topological properties may be computationally prohibitive or even impossible. Moreover, the increasing use of sensor networks in mission-critical applications further motivates restricted memory models, since these networks constitute of devices with small memory and low computing power.

The main focus of this book is to summarize the topological conditions which determine the feasibility of fault-tolerant consensus. Alternatively, we present studies on the determination of the class of networks that allow participants to reach consensus, and present protocols that solve the problem in these classes of networks. The results exactly determine the structure of networks that can optimally support the usage of fault-tolerant protocols and thus can be applied in the design of such networks. Another practical benefit of these studies is that using the outlined techniques, one can exactly determine the worst fault situations that can be tolerated in existing network infrastructures.

Dimitris Sakavalas and Lewis Tseng
April 2019

Acknowledgments

The completion of this book has been supported by Boston College. We would like to thank all authors who have contributed to the results presented in this book. We are indebted to our friends, colleagues, and research collaborators with whom we have had numerous joyful and meaningful discussions on the topics addressed in this book. These include Vartika Bhandari, Chris Litsas, Aris Pagourtzis, Giorgos Panagiotakos, Lili Su, and Nitin H. Vaidya.

We are grateful to the editor, Michel Raynal, and the referees, Hsin-Hao Su and Lili Su, for their detailed comments and suggestions which significantly improved the presentation and clarity of the book. Finally, we would like to thank Michel Raynal for his kind invitation to write a book for the Synthesis Lectures on Distributed Computing Theory series he is editing for Morgan & Claypool Publishers.

Dimitris Sakavalas and Lewis Tseng
April 2019

PART I

Network Topology and Fault-Tolerance

CHAPTER 1

Introduction

In the course of this first chapter, we will give formal definitions of all the notions and problems encountered in the rest of this work. For the fundamental notions about distributed systems, our presentation has been mainly affected by the standard textbooks of the field, namely, [6, 58, 80]. Although the book is addressed to graduate students in computer science or more experienced readers in the field, no prior knowledge on distributed systems is assumed.

1.1 COMPUTATIONAL MODEL

Distributed computing environments model the situation where several interacting entities, hereafter referred to as *processes*, cooperate to achieve a common goal/task in the absence of a central authority. In the *message-passing* framework, we assume that processes communicate by sending messages over communication channels in order to cooperate. The process set and the pattern of connections provided by the communication channels together describe the directed communication network $G = (V, E)$. The node set $V = \{1, \dots, n\}$ of G is identified with the process set, and the edge set E contains a directed edge (i, j) if and only if there is a communication channel between the processes i, j through which i can send messages to j. We also assume that each process can send messages to itself as well; however, for convenience, we exclude self-loops from set E. Whenever we refer to undirected networks, an edge (i, j) will denote an unordered pair representing a bidirectional channel. In the following, we will use the terms processes and nodes interchangeably since the notions coincide in the results presented. Observe that through the definition of V each process can be considered to be assigned a unique identifier i. That is, we consider the assignment of ids is fixed and given by the description of the network.

Processes will be modeled as interactive infinite-state machines as in [58]. The set of all interconnected processes is usually called the *distributed system*. We will focus on *static* networks, i.e., networks in which the sets of processes and edges do not change during an execution of the system. A configuration of the system is a vector comprising of the states of all processes and can be thought of as a snapshot of all the states at a certain point of the execution. A distributed algorithm is essentially the assignment of a state machine to each of the processes in the system.

Executions An *execution* or *run* of a distributed system is a complete description of the sequence of events happening in the system over time, i.e., sent messages, received messages, and configurations. Certain restrictions on the structure of this sequence are defined by the specific type of system being modeled. To justify the succession of events implied by the execution sequence, we assume an external source of "real time" that in general is not directly observable by the processes (cf. [37]). For the purpose of analysis, we assume that time proceeds in discrete *time steps*, i.e., there are only enumerable time-points.[1]

Events   Depending on processes' *speeds*, which are the frequencies with which the processes take local (computational) steps, at any time step, a subset of the processes is scheduled to take a local step. Each *local step* of a process i is comprised of the following local *events* which cause a state transition to the process i.

1. A *send* event $send(i, j, m)$ for each $j \in A$ where A is a subset of the outgoing neighbors of process i. Naturally, a $send(i, j, m)$ event results in the transmission of message m from process i to j.

2. A *receive* event $receive(j, i, m)$ for each $j \in A$ where A is a subset of the incoming neighbors of process i. Naturally, if process j sends message m to i at time step t, then the first occurrence of event $receive(j, i, m)$ after time t will result in the receipt of m by i.

3. A computation event $compute(i)$, which may include arbitrary computations similar to a sequential state machine, considering received messages as inputs.

   For the sake of simplicity, in the distributed computing literature, it is often assumed that local events take negligible time compared to a time step.

1.1.1   SYNCHRONY

There are two important timing notions associated with the execution of a system and concern the synchrony between the system components.

- The *message delivery delay*, which represents the amount of time steps that it takes for a message to be delivered, once it is sent. An upper bound d on message delivery delay implies that in the given execution all messages will be delivered within d time steps from their transmission.

- The *relative speeds* of processes, which is usually described by the *relative speed interval*, i.e., the minimum number of time steps k, such that during any sequence of k subsequent time steps, each process takes at least one local step.

As is common in the literature, we will focus on the following two extreme models regarding synchrony.

---

[1]A more general approach regarding time, used in [37, 80], is to assume that each process has access to a *local clock*, where a clock is a monotone nondecreasing function of real time.

Synchronous Model   In the *synchronous model*, we assume that the execution is partitioned into discrete *rounds*, which represent consecutive time intervals. The executions are restricted such that during each round, each process performs a send event, all messages sent in that round are delivered, and all processes perform local computations based on the received messages. Assuming known upper time bounds d, δ on delivery delay and the relative speed interval respectively, the simplest form of the synchronous model (also referred to as the fully synchronous model [80]) can be described by the property $d = \delta = 1$ and the duration of each round is 1 time step.

Observe that any synchronous algorithm can be adapted to the general case where bounds d, δ are arbitrary but known. This can trivially be achieved by letting each round have duration $(d + 1)\delta$ so that the first messages transmitted in every round will be received by the end of it.[2]

Asynchronous Model   In contrast, in the asynchronous model, no fixed bounds on the delays and relative process speeds are assumed to be known. Specifically, the delivery delay of messages is finite but no *a priori* known time bound is assumed on it. That is, a message sent through a channel will arrive at its destination within some finite but unpredictable time. Moreover, the speeds of processes may arbitrarily differ, i.e., the relative speed interval might be arbitrarily large, though finite. The above suggest that the only information that the processes can deduce will be due to the events they observe and their succession; because of this, algorithms in this model are said to be *event-driven*.

1.1.2   INPUTS AND OUTPUTS

Following the formulation of [58], we adopt the convention that processes' inputs and outputs are encoded in corresponding input and output variables in the states of the processes. Specifically, different inputs are encoded in the different start states, and the output of each process is placed in its designated *write-once* output variable. The outputs of the processes are also referred to as *decisions*. Essentially, as in the sequential model of computation, inputs and outputs are communicated between the processes and some external entity.[3]

1.1.3   INITIAL KNOWLEDGE OF PROCESSES

As is usual in the distributed computing literature, we assume that each process, due to its participation in the communication network, has some *a priori* local knowledge (e.g., about the network structure). Specifically, we assume that each process knows its id and the ids of its neighbors in the network. Variations of a more refined model, usually called the unknown network model, are considered in [6, 80] where each process has a number of ports, i.e., external connection points and every communication channel connects two ports at adjacent nodes. In that approach, a processor sends a message to its neighbor by loading it onto the appropriate

---

[2]Note that there exist better bounds for the duration of a round; their study is outside the scope of this book.

[3]In the more general formulation of the Universal Composability framework, presented in [17], this external entity is modeled by the *environment machine*.

port. Although the presented results are argued by referring to the id's of a process' neighbors, most of these results can trivially be adapted for the unknown network model.

Having assumed this basic level of knowledge as described above, in the following, when further initial knowledge is assumed, e.g., additional topological knowledge, it will be clearly stated in the description of the specific knowledge model studied. We assume that the initial knowledge of every process (including its id and the ids of its neighbors) is provided to it as a part of its initial input information.[4] Whenever the distinction between the knowledge and the input value of a process is necessary we will refer to them as *initial knowledge* and *initial input value*, respectively. These two components constitute the input of a process.

1.2   ADVERSARY MODEL

In *fault-tolerant* distributed computing, the goal is to design distributed protocols that achieve a certain task even if some of the system's components do not execute the protocol as expected. A typical such example is the case in which processes crash and stop executing. In a given execution of a distributed algorithm, a process is called *faulty* or *corrupted* if its behavior deviates from the one specified by the algorithm. Clearly, the worst case of such misbehavior occurs when faulty processes coordinate their actions. To model such a worst-case scenario, it is assumed that the actions of faulty processes are coordinated centrally by an external entity which corrupts them, called the *adversary*.

One can easily observe that if the adversary can corrupt any subset of processes and make them misbehave in any way, then the achievement of most meaningful distributed tasks becomes impossible or vague. Thus, fault-tolerance studies assume different restrictions on the adversary which are determined by the *adversary model*. More concretely, the adversary model specifies the sets of processes that can be (simultaneously) corrupted by the adversary, i.e., the *corruptible* or *feasible fault* sets, as well as the way in which a faulty process can deviate from the behavior specified by the algorithm (*corruption type*). Moreover, the time in which the adversary is allowed to corrupt processes also affects the correctness of solutions and thus the adversary model also specifies this parameter.

1.2.1   CORRUPTIBLE SETS

The most common restriction on the corruptible sets is described by the *threshold* or *global adversary* model introduced in the seminal works of [50, 78]. In this model a fixed upper bound f is imposed on the overall number of faulty processes in the network. In contrast, in the *local adversary* model introduced by Koo in [45], the adversary can corrupt at most f incoming neighbors (denoted by N_i^-) of any node i. Finally, the *general adversary model*, introduced in [40], encompasses all known adversary models with respect to the definition of corruptible

---

[4]From an algorithmic point of view, this means that the initial knowledge of the processes in the context of a specific knowledge model can be modeled as a part of their input in any algorithm considered in the specific model.

sets; the corruptible sets are described explicitly by a family of process sets $\mathcal{F}$. We summarize the definitions of the models below.

- **Global adversary model:** Given a given bound $f \in \mathbb{N}$ with $f \leq n$, for every corruptible set F it holds that $|F| \leq f$.

- **Local adversary model:** Given a given bound $f \in \mathbb{N}$ with $f \leq n$, for every corruptible set F it holds that for every $i \in V, |F \cap N_i^-| \leq f$.

- **General adversary model:** An *adversary structure* (or *fault domain*) $\mathcal{F}$ for the set of processes V is a monotone family of subsets of V, i.e., $\mathcal{F} \subseteq 2^V$, where all subsets of a set F are in $\mathcal{F}$ if $F \in \mathcal{F}$. In this adversary model, given an adversary structure $\mathcal{F}$, a process set F is corruptible only if $F \in \mathcal{F}$.

The majority of the results presented in this book concern the global adversary model; the local and the general adversary models will be considered in Chapters 7 and 8, respectively.

1.2.2   CORRUPTION TYPE

The strongest case of corruption is to allow the adversary full control over the corrupted processes. In addition, the adversary is *omniscient*, i.e., it knows the specification of algorithms and internal states and messages exchanged by fault-free processes. This models situations in which the corresponding corrupted players might arbitrarily misbehave. However, there are many cases in which the misbehavior of players is limited and can be described by specifying a restricted set of (misbehaving) actions. In the following, we describe the two most common corruption types studied in the literature, on which we will focus on the rest of the book.

- **Crash failure model:** In this corruption type, the adversary is allowed to make a corrupted process crash at any point of the execution, i.e., make the process stop executing the protocol from that point on. A faulty process behaves correctly up to the point it crashes. Hence, the model is also called fail-stop failure model.

- **Byzantine failure model:** In this case, the adversary fully controls the process and can make it misbehave arbitrarily from the protocol, e.g., by arbitrarily changing its state or sending different erroneous messages to each neighbor.

All the processes that are not corrupted are called *fault-free* in our discussion. Algorithms that cope with crash and Byzantine faults will be called *crash-tolerant* and *Byzantine-tolerant*, respectively.

1.2.3   CORRUPTION TIME

As already mentioned, the adversary model also specifies the point in time when the adversary is allowed to corrupt processes. We distinguish two types of adversaries regarding this parameter.

- **Static adversary:** This type of adversary must perform all corruptions before the protocol execution, i.e., the set of corrupted players is fixed (but typically unknown) during the whole execution.

- **Adaptive adversary:** In this case, the adversary can corrupt processes at any point during the execution, possibly depending on information which he obtained up to this point. Note that once a process is corrupted, it remains corrupted until the end of the execution. Specifically, an adaptive adversary can corrupt additional processes during the execution as long as the overall set of faults does not violate the corruptible sets restrictions imposed by the model.

Clearly, a static adversary represents a weaker adversary than the adaptive one. All algorithms presented in this book, solve the respective problems under the existence of both an adaptive and a static adversary.

1.3 CONSENSUS PROBLEMS

In this section, we define the consensus problem and its variations studied in this book. Intuitively, the goal is to achieve agreement of processes to a common value despite the existence of faulty processes in the system. The basic variation of the problem was introduced in [50] and it has been proven one of the most fundamental problems in distributed computing.

Note that it is common in the fault-tolerance literature to refer to the output of a process as its *decision*. When we require a condition to hold after any finite amount of time, we will just state that we require that the condition *eventually* holds. In all of the following consensus variations, the processes start the execution with initial input values from a particular value set X at the same time.

Binary and Multi-valued Consensus   The simple class of consensus problems in which $|X| = 2$ (typically $X = \{0, 1\}$) has been given special attention in the literature and problems in this class are called *binary consensus* variations. On the other hand, the *multi-valued consensus* variations correspond to the case where $|X| > 2$. Binary consensus variations are interesting because a solution to a binary consensus problem usually implies a solution to the corresponding multi-valued one with a small overhead in round and communication complexity, compared to the size of X (e.g., [22]).

1.3.1 EXACT CONSENSUS

To avoid confusion with the other variations studied, we will refer to the original problem as *exact consensus*. Since a Byzantine adversary is strictly stronger than the one in the crash failure case, it is common to give different definitions for the problem in those two models.

Definition 1.1 Exact Crash-Tolerant Consensus.   We say that an algorithm achieves exact crash-tolerant consensus if the following conditions hold.

1. *Agreement:* No two processes output different values.

2. *Validity:* Any output value of a process equals the input value of a process.

3. *Termination:* Every fault-free process eventually outputs a value x.

Definition 1.2 Exact Byzantine-Tolerant Consensus. We say that an algorithm achieves exact Byzantine-tolerant consensus if the following conditions hold.

1. *Agreement:* No two fault-free processes output different values.

2. *Validity:* Any output value for a fault-free process equals the input value of a fault-free process.

3. *Termination:* Every fault-free process eventually outputs a value x.

Notice that the agreement condition is weaker in the Byzantine case, as we cannot require a Byzantine faulty process to output the same value as a fault-free one since the first makes arbitrary state transitions dictated by the adversary. Regarding validity, the requirement is stronger in the Byzantine case. This is due to the fact that allowing the output value of fault-free processes to be the input of any process would mean that all outputs may be equal to a faulty value, falsely reported by a Byzantine process.

Observation on Multivalued Consensus Usually in the case of multivalued Byzantine consensus, the validity property is replaced with a weaker version, namely:

- *Weak Validity* [48]: If all fault-free processes have the same input, then the output of every fault-free process equals its input.

This is because Gil Niger [72] proved that to achieve strong validity (the original validity property), the number of processes has to be greater or equal to $3|X| + 1$, which is unlikely to hold in practical systems if X contains many elements.

FLP Impossibility Result The impossibility of consensus with one crash fault in asynchronous systems, proved in [31], constitutes one of the fundamental results in distributed computing. The need to overcome this impossibility has led to the definition of weaker versions of the problem. To circumvent the impossibility, the literature has been largely focused on the *approximate consensus* and *randomized consensus* problems which relax specific requirements of the original problem. In this work we will also focus in the approximate consensus problem and its variations.

1.3.2 APPROXIMATE AND ASYMPTOTIC CONSENSUS

In many real-life systems, agreement on the exact same value by all processes is not required or is even impossible. It is thus natural to require that the processes roughly agree on the same value. This problem has been mainly presented in two variations called *approximate consensus* and *asymptotic consensus* which have important practical applications in areas ranging from sensor fusion [11] and load balancing [23], to natural systems like flocking [99] and opinion dynamics [39].

We first give the definition of the approximate consensus problem, introduced in [28]. In this problem, all processes have real-valued inputs, i.e., $X = \mathbb{R}$, and are required to output values in $\mathbb{R}$. Ignoring the bit complexity, it is assumed that the processes can send real-valued data in messages; in practice, all of the approximate and asymptotic consensus algorithms presented in this book work if we restrict to the case of $X = \mathbb{Q}$. Unlike the exact consensus problem, in approximate consensus, the processes are not required to agree exactly on a value, but rather agree on values that are in distance $\epsilon > 0$ from each other.

Definition 1.3 Approximate Consensus. We say that an algorithm achieves approximate consensus if it satisfies the following conditions for any $\epsilon > 0$.

1. *ϵ-Agreement (or Convergence)*: The output values of any pair of fault-free processes are within ϵ of each other.

2. *Validity*: The output of any fault-free process is within the range (convex hull) of the inputs of the fault-free processes.

3. *Termination*: All fault-free processes eventually output a value $x \in \mathbb{R}$.

In the *asymptotic consensus* problem, the termination requirement is omitted and the processes are not required to output a (single) value. Instead, in this case, each process i is assumed to maintain a real state value $v_i[t] \in \mathbb{R}$, for $t \in \mathbb{N}$, which is updated regularly, with $v_i[0]$ denoting the real-valued input of process i.

Value $v_i[t]$ in general represents the t-th update of the state value; we will also refer to it as the state value of i in *iteration t*. Technically, in synchronous systems, it is usually assumed that a process updates its state value in every round and thus, $v_i[t]$ is the state value of process i in round t. On the other hand, in asynchronous systems, i updates the value every time it observes a certain event (depending on the algorithm) thus creating the sequence $(v_i[t])_{t \in \mathbb{N}}$. Let $M[t], m[t]$ be the maximum and the minimum state at fault-free processes in iteration t. The definition of asymptotic consensus follows.

Definition 1.4 Asymptotic Consensus. We say that an algorithm achieves asymptotic consensus if it satisfies the following conditions.

1. *Agreement (or Convergence)*: The state values of any pair of fault-free processes converge to the same value, i.e., $\lim_{t \to \infty} M[t] - m[t] = 0$.

2. *Validity*: The state values of any fault-free process are within the range of the inputs of the fault-free processes, i.e., $\forall t > 0, M[t] \leq M[0]$ and $m[t] \geq m[0]$.

Observe that equivalently the convergence condition can be stated as:

$$\forall \epsilon > 0, \text{ there exists an iteration } t_\epsilon \text{ such that for } t \geq t_\epsilon, M[t] - m[t] < \epsilon.$$

Relation between Approximate and Asymptotic Consensus   Essentially, asymptotic consensus is a weaker variation of approximate consensus, not requiring termination. Conversely, most asymptotic consensus algorithms presented in the literature can easily be converted to an approximate consensus algorithm. More specifically, as observed in [58], each process can locally compute an upper bound for the number of iterations t_ϵ needed for convergence, and thus terminate after that.

All the approximate consensus algorithms presented in this book are essentially algorithms achieving asymptotic consensus in which we can also guarantee termination of processes. More details on the transformation of a given asymptotic consensus solution to a solution for approximate consensus can be found in [28, 44, 58].

1.4   ALGORITHM CONSTRAINTS

General algorithms for solving the aforementioned problems are naturally described by the computational model, presented in Section 1.1, and are also called *round based algorithms*. These algorithms comprise of the following three *steps* as implied by the local step notion defined in Section 1.1.

- *Send step*: The process sends messages to its neighbors according to a message rule.

- *Receive step*: The process receives messages from a subset of its neighbors.

- *Compute step*: The process modifies its state according to the messages it received in the receive phase.

We will also focus on the specific class of *iterative approximate consensus algorithms (IAC)*, which provide appropriate solutions for the asymptotic and approximate consensus problems. In this class of algorithms, each process maintains a special real state value v, which after a sufficient number of rounds, becomes its *output*. Moreover, it is assumed that processes in IAC algorithms are *memory-less*, i.e., only maintain the information (state value) from the current round and not any information obtained in previous rounds. We will distinguish between the synchronous and asynchronous cases by giving the appropriate class definitions for each model. Additionally, we give an adaptation of these algorithms (presented in Section 6.1), suitable for the setting where the topology knowledge of processes and the *relay depth*, i.e., the maximum number of hops any message can be relayed, are restricted.

IAC algorithms are of specific interest because of their low requirements in terms of memory and amount of multi-hop message relays compared to the general ones. For instance, a process executing an IAC algorithm only maintains a real state value at each point of the execution and no knowledge of the topology is assumed. Moreover, messages are only transmitted to and received from the immediate neighborhood and no message relay takes place. These two properties are useful, particularly in large-scale networks, in order to avoid memory overload and network congestion, respectively.

1.4.1   SYNCHRONOUS IAC ALGORITHMS

In the synchronous case, a process updates its state value in every round depending on the state values received by all its incoming neighbors and its own state; we remind that typically, a process i can send its state to itself; thus, this is included in the multi-set $R_i[t]$ in the receive step of the algorithm. Note that $v_i[0]$ represents the initial input state value of process i. The structure of the algorithms is presented below.

Synchronous IAC Algorithm

Each process i performs the following three steps in every round t.

- *Transmit step*: Transmit current state value, namely $v_i[t - 1]$, to all outgoing neighbors and i.

- *Receive step*: Receive state values from all incoming neighbors and i. Denote by $R_i[t]$ the multi-set of state values that process i received at round t.

- *Update step*: Update state using a transition (or update) function Z_i, where Z_i is a part of the specification of the algorithm, and takes as input the set $R_i[t]$. Let the function $mean(A)$ be a *weighted mean* of the elements in a multi-set A. Then the update is performed through function Z_i which is of the following form:

$$v_i[p] := Z_i(R_i[t]) = mean(R_i[t]).$$

Considering the weights of the weighted mean to be 0 for some elements of R allows to completely discard these elements from R. In previous works (e.g., [28, 44, 58]), this case has been handled through a *selection(A)* function which returned a multi-set B, a subset of multiset A.

1.4.2   ASYNCHRONOUS IAC ALGORITHMS

In asynchronous systems, the notion of a round is usually replaced with that of an event-oriented *phase*. The beginning and the end of a specific phase for a certain process depends on well-defined local events that the process can observe rather than on a notion of time that is implied in synchronous systems. Consequently, processes may execute certain phases in different real-time points.

In the asynchronous version of IAC algorithms, the messages containing the states are also tagged with the phase index to which the states correspond. Moreover, each process i waits to receive only a certain number of messages m containing states from phase $p - 1$ before computing the new state in its p-th phase. We stress that m may be a function of the number of processes n and the maximum number of corruptions f, defined in the global adversary model. Due to message delays and varying speeds, different processes may potentially perform their p-th phase at very different real times. Note that $v_i[0]$ represents the initial input state value of process i.

Asynchronous IAC algorithm

Each process i performs the following three steps in (asynchronous) phase t.

- *Transmit step*: Transmit messages of the form $(v_i[p - 1], p - 1)$ to all the outgoing neighbors and i; where $v_i[p - 1]$ is the current state value, which is accompanied by the *phase tag $p - 1$*, indicating the corresponding phase.

- *Receive step*: Wait until receiving at least $m \leq n$ messages from m distinct incoming neighbors, including i. Denote by $R_i[p]$ the set of messages that process i received at phase p.

- *Update step*: Update state using a transition (or update) function Z_i, where Z_i is a part of the specification of the algorithm, and takes as input the set $R_i[p]$, i.e.,

$$v_i[p] := Z_i(R_i[t]) = mean(R_i[t]).$$

The *mean* function is as defined in Section 1.4.1.

1.4.3 COMPARISON OF GENERAL AND ITERATIVE ALGORITHMS

The class of IAC algorithms may seem highly related with the general ones, since they maintain the *transmit, receive, and update* structure. Nevertheless, the classes present important differences summarized below.

- In general algorithms, processes can maintain and exchange arbitrary information. On the other hand, in IAC algorithms, the processes only exchange their real valued states and their state update is restricted to be a weighted mean of the last states received.

- In IAC algorithms, a process i proceeds to its state update whenever a very simple condition holds, i.e., it receives a certain number of messages-states m from its neighbors. In contrast, in general algorithms, a process may proceed to a local update of its state whenever an arbitrary predicate holds; typically this will be included in its local arbitrary compute step.

- Intuitively, in IAC algorithms, no routing of values occurs between processes in the graph that are not immediate neighbors. Observe that by the definition of the IAC update step, a process only sends to its neighbors the weighted mean of the values of neighbors received in a previous step. This, in an arbitrary graph, prohibits values to be propagated in h steps between processes with distance h and thus, values cannot be communicated between non-neighboring processes. Instead, in general algorithms, information can be routed throughout the whole graph from a process to others not in its neighborhood. This allows to simulate more communication channels between processes, which proves to reduce the round complexity of approximate consensus.

General algorithms usually achieve consensus more efficiently in terms of round complexity, e.g., [6, 49, 58, 78]; however, they require extra information and overhead, such as topology knowledge and routing mechanism. Therefore, iterative algorithms have been also extensively studied. Byzantine fault-tolerant iterative consensus has been explored in both complete and undirected graphs, e.g., [1, 6, 28, 30, 58]. Using iterative algorithms to achieve fault-free consensus [12, 42] and approximate consensus in a restricted fault model [51–53, 101] have been studied extensively as well.

1.5   SUMMARY OF RESULTS

Considering the different models, algorithm class choices, and consensus problems, we present the summary of work mainly focused on directed networks. As will be seen in Chapter 2, tight conditions on undirected networks for solving different types of consensus problems have been identified and are presented in Table 2.1. In addition, the tight condition for solving approximate crash-tolerant consensus in synchronous systems follows from the decentralized control literature [12, 42]. More recent work presented in this book addresses exact and approximate consensus in synchronous and asynchronous systems under the crash and Byzantine failure model. Table 1.1 summarizes results on consensus in directed networks and open problems in this area, and can be used as reference to the works and the corresponding chapters of this book where the related results are presented.

Moreover in Chapter 6, we present results of [84, 86], considering the effect of topology knowledge and relay depth on the feasibility of approximate crash-tolerant, and Byzantine tolerant consensus, respectively.

In Chapters 7 and 8, we present topological conditions related with the feasibility of consensus under different adversary models. Specifically, in Chapter 7, we present the results of [73, 89]; these works address the *Reliable Broadcast* problem under a local adversary and the *ad hoc* network model, where the topological knowledge of processes is restricted to their immediate neighborhood. Due to the relation between the problems, the presented topological conditions affecting the solvability of reliable broadcast can easily be extended to conditions related with the feasibility of exact consensus.

Table 1.1: Summary of recent results on directed networks

Fault Model	System	Output	General Algorithm	Iterative Algorithm
Crash	Synthronous (Chapter 3)	Exact	[93]	
		Approximate	Follows from [12, 42]	
	Asynchronous (Chapter 4)	Approximate	[93]	[87]
Byzantine (Chapter 5)	Synthronous	Exact	[93]	Open
		Approximate	[86]	[98]
	Asynchronous	Approximate	Open	[98]

Finally, in Chapter 8 we present topological conditions related with the feasibility of consensus and the reliable message transmission problems under different adversary models. Specifically we present the results of [74, 94] that consider the *general adversary model*, introduced in [40]. Similarly with the case of reliable broadcast, the feasibility of consensus and reliable message transmission are also related.

1.6   RELATED WORK

For completeness, we discuss two categories of closely related work. Note that this section is by no means a comprehensive survey, as consensus is still an active research topic. Please refer to well-known textbooks (e.g., [6, 58, 81, 82]) for classical results and our survey [88] for some recent works.

1.6.1   RELATED PROBLEMS IN INCOMPLETE NETWORKS

Undirected Networks   Shortly after Lamport, Shostak, and Pease addressed the Byzantine consensus problem in complete networks [50, 78], two subsequent papers independently [26, 30] characterized the necessary and sufficient conditions for Byzantine consensus in undirected networks. Bansal et al. [10] identified tight conditions for achieving Byzantine consensus in undirected networks using authentication. In Chapter 2, we briefly discuss why results in undirected work do not directly apply to directed networks.

Control Systems Literature   Consensus is also an important problem in the decentralized control area. Bertsekas and Tsitsiklis [12] and Jadbabaei, Lin, and Morse [42] explored reaching approximate consensus in the absence of faults. In their work, the communication graph may be partially connected and time-varying. In general-directed networks, LeBlanc et al. [53, 54] and Zhang and Sundaram [101, 102] developed results for iterative algorithms for approximate consensus under a *weaker* fault model, where a Byzantine faulty process must send identical messages to all the neighbors. Under the same model, Dibaji et al. studied how to solve quantized consensus using a randomized strategy [25].

Dynamic Networks   Recently, researchers have explored fault-tolerant consensus problems in directed dynamic networks. The typical fault model in this line of work is *message adversary*, and all the processes are assumed to be fault-free in [14]. The message adversary controls the communication pattern. In other words, the adversary has the power to specify the sets of communication graphs in each round. Biely et al. studied the k-set consensus problem (i.e., at most k different outputs at fault-free processes) in dynamic networks, and the system is assumed to be synchronous [14]. Charron-Bost et al. considered the approximate consensus problem in dynamic networks [19]. In 2018, Függer et al. obtained the tight bounds for asymptotic and approximate consensus in dynamic networks [35], and studied the multi-dimensional consensus [34].

1.6.2   RECENT PROGRESS

Asynchronous Consensus   Due to FLP impossibility result [30], dealing with consensus in asynchronous settings led to additional model assumptions and weaker versions of the consensus problem in order to achieve feasibility. There are three main directions.

- *Failure detectors*: For crash-tolerant consensus, Chandra et al. proposed using failure detectors to solve the problem [18]. Mostéfaoui and Raynal later proposed a notion called *leader oracle*, and then showed how it can be used to solve asynchronous consensus [68]. For Byzantine consensus, Mostéfaoui and Raynal proposed a framework based on quorums and unreliable failure detectors [67]. Baldoni et al. examined how to use two types of failure detectors to solve asynchronous Byzantine consensus [8]. Some important fundamental tradeoffs under different types of oracles were identified in [36].

- *Condition-based approach*: Mostéfaoui et al. [62] identified that under some combinations of input vectors, it is possible to solve consensus in asynchronous systems even if there are faulty processes. A series of works by the same authors followed, which focused on using condition-based approaches to solve various type of consensus problems, e.g., [63–65]. Mostéfaoui et al. later combined failure detectors and the condition-based approach to solve the k-set agreement problem [66]. For Byzantine consensus, Friedman et al. [33] proposed a condition-base algorithm.

- *Randomized algorithms*: In 2015, Mostéfaoui et al. proposed a randomized Byzantine consensus algorithm that has $O(n^2)$ message complexity and the expected number of rounds to terminate is constant [61]. In 2018, Bangalore et al. [9] proposed a randomized Byzantine consensus protocol with improved expected running time and local computations complexity. Their algorithms have the *almost-surely terminating* property, i.e., the algorithm terminates with probability 1.

Multi-Valued Consensus   In the original *exact* Byzantine consensus problem [50, 78], both inputs and outputs of processes are binary values. In subsequent works [57, 95], the authors proposed the multi-valued version of consensus, in which the inputs may take more than two *real* values. Recently, multi-valued consensus received renewed attentions and researchers proposed algorithms that achieve asymptotically optimal communication complexity (number of bits transmitted) under different assumptions [32, 55, 75–77]. For the asynchronous multi-valued consensus problem, Mostéfaoui and Raynal developed an algorithm minimizing the total number of messages [69, 71], and an algorithm that has the *intrusion-tolerant* property [70]—if all the faulty processes propose the same value v, while no fault-free processes proposes it, then v cannot be the output.

Multi-Dimensional Input/Output   In the Byzantine vector consensus (or multi-dimensional consensus) [59, 97], each process is given a d-dimensional vector of reals as its input ($d \geq 1$), and the output is also a d-dimensional vector. In complete networks, the recent papers by Mendes and Herlihy [59] and Vaidya and Garg [97] addressed approximate vector consensus in the presence of Byzantine faults. Subsequent work by Vaidya [96] explored the problem in incomplete *directed* graphs. Later, Tseng and Vaidya [91] proposed the convex hull consensus problem, in which fault-free processes have to agree on a "largest possible" polytope in the d-dimensional space that may not necessarily be equal to a d-dimensional vector (a single point).

Partial Synchrony   Another line of work explores more elaborate synchrony assumptions. Alistarh et al. studied k-set consensus in partially synchronous systems [3]. Milosevic et al. considered permanent and transient transmission faults in a variation of partially synchronous systems [60]. Hamouma et al. [38] studied the consensus problem when only a few links may be synchronous throughout the execution of the algorithm.

The fundamental properties of partial synchrony were identified in three separate works. In [83], Raynal and Stainer examined the relation between message adversaries and failure detectors in asynchronous systems. In [2], Alistarh et al. addressed a fundamental question of partial synchrony: "For how long does the system need to be synchronous to solve crash-tolerant consensus?" Bouzid et al. [16] studied a related problem—how many eventually synchronous links are necessary for achieving consensus?

CHAPTER 2

Consensus and Network Topology

The main goal of this work is to present an extensive overview of the relation between the network topology and the feasibility of consensus. In this chapter, we will introduce some basic graph notions to facilitate our study and will focus on the topological conditions that render the corresponding problems solvable. Moreover, the intuition behind the way that topology affects the feasibility of consensus will be discussed. Regarding the adversary, the prime focus of this book will be the global threshold model. As will be made evident, the study of fault-tolerant network topologies in this simple model gives a useful intuition toward extending the results to other adversary models.

Consensus variations in message-passing networks have been extensively studied in undirected complete (e.g., [1, 28, 29, 49, 78]) and incomplete graphs (e.g., [26, 30]). The tight conditions on undirected graphs identified in the literature are summarized in Table 2.1. In this case, the topological conditions affecting consensus feasibility are defined in terms of the *node connectivity* [100] of the graph. Recently, significant efforts [20, 51–53, 86, 93, 98, 101] have been devoted to determine the topological conditions that render consensus variations solvable in *incomplete directed networks*, where communication channels are not necessarily bi-directional. In this book, we will mainly focus on the general case of directed networks and analyze how their topology affects consensus feasibility.

In the rest of the chapter, we first discuss in detail the results of Table 2.1 on undirected networks and identify why these results do not directly apply to directed networks. In the second part, we present the topological conditions pertinent to the directed network case and briefly discuss the intuition behind the conditions' tightness.

2.1 THE UNDIRECTED NETWORK CASE

We next present the topological conditions that have been proved necessary and sufficient for the feasibility of consensus variations in undirected graphs and outline the validity of the respective theorems. The key point concerning the sufficiency of the conditions is that if the respective connectivity conditions hold, then one can implement a subroutine of *Reliable Message Transmission* (RMT) to simulate a reliable channel between every pair of processes (cf. [27]). Reliable message transmission is the problem of achieving correct delivery of a message m from a sender-

Table 2.1: Tight conditions for undirected networks with a global adversary

	Crash-Tolerant Consensus	**Byzantine Consensus**
Synthronous	$(f + 1)$-connectivity, $n > f$ (follow from well-known results [58, 6])	$(2f + 1)$-connectivity, $n > 3f$ ([30, 26])
Asynchronous (Approximate Consensus)	$(f + 1)$-connectivity, $n > 2f$ (follow from well-known results [58, 6])	$(2f + 1)$-connectivity, $n > 3f$ (from [1, 30])

process s to a receiver-process r even if some of the other processes are corrupted and misbehave from the given protocol. The formal definition of the problem follows.

Definition 2.1   Reliable Message Transmission (RMT).   We assume the existence of a designated process $s \in V$, called the *sender*, who wants to propagate a certain value $x_s \in X$, where X is the initial message space, to a designated process r, called the *receiver*. We say that a distributed protocol achieves (or solves) RMT if by the end of the protocol the receiver r has *decided on x_s*, i.e., if it has been able to output the value x_s originally sent by the sender.

Most consensus algorithms in complete networks require reliable communication channels between every pair of processes; since the connectivity condition allows to simulate a virtual complete network, a solution for incomplete networks can be obtained by employing any protocol for complete networks and an RMT subroutine for all message transmissions.

Since we are interested in process failures, we will rely on the notion of node connectivity. With $conn(G)$ we denote the minimum number of nodes whose removal results in either a disconnected graph or a trivial 1-node graph. Graph G is said to be c-connected if $conn(G) \geq c$. Observe that removal of up to any $c - 1$ nodes does not cause a c-connected graph to become disconnected. We will often use the terms *graph* and *network* interchangeably.

2.1.1   SYNCHRONOUS NETWORKS

Theorem 2.2   *Exact crash-tolerant consensus in synchronous systems is possible if and only if $conn(G) > f$ and $n > f$.*

Proof Sketch: We first show the impossibility of consensus in the case where the conditions do not hold. The bound $n > f$ is trivial to see by definition of the problem. We can easily see that if $conn(G) \leq f$, consensus is impossible since the condition implies that there exists a separator S of the graph of size $\geq f$. Assume that the separator disconnects the graph in two components with node-sets L, R and all processes in L have input m and all processes in R have input $M \neq m$. In an execution where the separator S is corrupted at the beginning of the protocol, no communication is possible between sets L, R. Thus, due to the validity requirement, all nodes in set L will output m and all nodes in R will output M which violates the agreement requirement.

We next outline a simple algorithm that achieves consensus whenever $n > f$ and $conn(G) \geq f + 1$ hold. Observe that by Menger's theorem [100], it holds that there are at least $f + 1$ node-disjoint paths between every pair of nodes i, j. One can hence simulate reliable message transmission (RMT) from i to j by running the following RMT protocol:

Crash-RMT: Process i sends the message along $f + 1$ node-disjoint paths to j and j decides on any value it receives first. Since one path will always be solely comprised of fault-free nodes, j will correctly receive the message and can decide on it; it is trivial to see that j will receive a value in at most $|V| = n$ synchronous rounds since this is an upper bound on the length of all paths. Since only crash faults are considered, no incorrect messages will be transmitted to j.

Subsequently, consensus can be solved by simulating any crash-tolerant consensus algorithm for complete graphs that assumes the existence of reliable channel, e.g., [58]. □

Theorem 2.3   *Exact Byzantine consensus in synchronous systems is possible if and only if $conn(G) > 2f$ and $n > 3f$.*

Proof Sketch: First it is trivial to argue for the impossibility of the case $n \leq 3f$. It is well known from [50, 78] that $n > 3f$ processes are required to solve consensus in a complete graph. If there existed a consensus algorithm for incomplete graphs with $n \leq 3f$, then the same algorithm could also be executed in an n-node complete graph and solve consensus, a contradiction.

Next we show that if $conn(G) \leq 2f$, then consensus is impossible. Since $conn(G) \leq 2f$ there must exist a separator S of the graph with $|S| \leq 2f$. Thus, S can be partitioned in sets F, C for which $|F|, |C| \leq f$. Assume that separator S disconnects graph G to components with node-sets L, R. Also assume an execution where the processes in F are all faulty (this is possible due to $|F| \leq f$), and the processes in sets L, C, R are fault-free. Consider the case where all the processes in L have input m, and all the processes in $R \cup C$ have input M, where $m \neq M$. Suppose that the processes in F (if $F \neq \emptyset$) behave to processes in L as if processes in $R \cup C \cup F$ have input m, while behaving to processes in R as if processes in $L \cup C \cup F$ have input M.[1]

Consider processes in L. Denote with N_L the set of fault-free neighbors of L. Since $C \cup F$ disconnects sets L, R and all nodes in f are fault free, it must hold that $N_L \subseteq C$ and, thus, L has at most f fault-free neighbors. Therefore, processes in L cannot distinguish between the following two scenarios:

- all the processes in N_L (if non-empty) are faulty, the rest of the processes are fault-free, and all the fault-free processes have input m; and

---

[1]This kind of attack is often used in the literature. The reader can address the proof of Theorem 7.8, where an analogous behavior of the faulty set is considered and is typically shown to be well defined.

- all the processes in F (if non-empty) are faulty, the rest of the processes are fault-free, and fault-free processes have input either m or M.

In the first scenario, for validity, the output of processes in L must be m. Therefore, in the second scenario as well, the output at the processes in L must be m. We can similarly show that the output at the processes in R must be M. Thus, if condition $conn(G) > 2f$ is not satisfied, processes in L and R can be forced to decide on different values, violating the agreement property. This completes the proof that the conjunction of conditions $n > 3f$ and $conn(G) > 2f$ is necessary for achieving consensus.

We next show that the conjunction of the conditions is also sufficient by outlining an algorithm that achieves consensus whenever they both hold. Since $conn(G) > 2f$, by Menger's Theorem, it holds that there are at least $2f + 1$ node-disjoint paths between any two nodes in G. This allows for the simulation of a reliable communication channel between any pair of nodes i and j by implementing the following RMT protocol.

Byzantine-RMT: Process i sends the message along $2f + 1$ node-disjoint paths between itself and j. Node j will decide on a message m if it receives the same message from at least $f + 1$ node-disjoint paths. Since there are at most f faulty processes, the messages received by j along a majority of these paths must be correct if i is fault-free. Moreover, if i is fault-free, then clearly j will receive the correct value in at most n synchronous rounds since n is an upper bound on the length of all paths. On the other hand, to guarantee the termination of the RMT protocol in the case where i is faulty, we assume that j decides on a default value $\perp$ if it hasn't received $f + 1$ copies of the same value from disjoint paths y round n.

Once we have reliable communication between all pairs of fault-free processes, we can solve consensus just by simulating any algorithm that solves the problem in an n-node complete graph that assumes reliable channel, e.g., [50, 78]. The latter is possible due to the fact that $n > 3f$. □

An alternate proof can be found in [30].

2.1.2 ASYNCHRONOUS NETWORKS

Since by [31] exact consensus is impossible even with one faulty process in asynchronous systems, we present and discuss the undirected network topological conditions related to approximate consensus here. As we will see the connectivity requirements do not change in the case of asynchronous networks; this is due to the fact that the aforementioned RMT protocols can be slightly modified to be executed in asynchronous networks, requiring the same connectivity.

Theorem 2.4 *Approximate crash-tolerant consensus in asynchronous systems is possible if and only if* $conn(G) \geq f + 1$ *and* $n > 2f$.

Proof Sketch: For complete graphs, the impossibility of approximate consensus for $n \leq 2f$ is presented in [58] and a matching algorithm is presented in [5]. The impossibility obviously also holds in incomplete undirected networks, else the incomplete network algorithm could be used to achieve approximate consensus in a complete graph. The impossibility of approximate consensus in the case of $conn(G) \leq f$ can be shown with similar arguments to the corresponding proof of Theorem 2.2.

A matching algorithm can be constructed by adapting an algorithm for complete networks that assumes reliable channel, e.g., [5]. Observe that protocol *Crash-RMT* presented in the proof of Theorem 2.2 is event-driven and, thus, its correctness is not affected by the asynchrony of the network. That is, process j will receive a message at some point from process i if i is fault-free. □

Theorem 2.5 *Approximate Byzantine consensus in asynchronous systems if possible if and only if $conn(G) \geq 2f + 1$ and $n > 3f$.*

Proof Sketch: For complete graphs, the impossibility for $n \leq 3f$ is proved in [30] and a matching algorithm can be found in [1]. As argued in Theorem 2.2, this impossibility holds for the undirected incomplete network case. The impossibility of approximate consensus in the case of $conn(G) \leq 2f$ can be shown with similar arguments to the corresponding proof of Theorem 2.3. To simulate reliable communication channels in this case observe that protocol *Byzantine-RMT* presented in the proof of Theorem 2.3 is event-driven and, thus, its correctness is not affected by the asynchrony of the network. That is, process j will receive a message from $f + 1$ node-disjoint paths such that all processes are fault-free on these paths at some point from process i if i is fault-free. □

2.2   THE DIRECTED NETWORK CASE

In this section, we discuss the complications arising for consensus, from the consideration of directed networks. We briefly discuss why the tight conditions on undirected networks (Table 2.1) do not easily generalize to directed networks. We will focus on the case of exact crash-tolerant consensus problem in synchronous systems. The cases of other consensus problems are left as exercises.

From Table 2.1, we know that $(f + 1)$-connectivity, and $n > f$ are together necessary and sufficient for achieving consensus [6, 58] in undirected network case. There are two straightforward ways to generalize the notion of undirected network connectivity to the case of a directed network.

- $(f + 1)$-*weak connectivity* [100]: removing up to f processes, the remaining graph is weakly connected.

  A directed graph is weakly connected if in the graph, any node is reachable from any other node by traversing edges in some direction (not necessarily in the direction of the edge). It should be obvious to see that weak connectivity is necessary, since processes need to exchange some information in order to achieve consensus. However, $(f + 1)$-weak connectivity is not sufficient for crash-tolerant consensus. Consider the network in Figure 2.1.

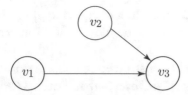

Figure 2.1: A weakly connected network where consensus is impossible.

Consensus is impossible to achieve even if $f = 0$ (every node is fault-free), since processes v_1 and v_2 cannot observe any common information.

- $(f + 1)$-*strong connectivity* [100]: removing up to f nodes, the remaining graph is strongly connected.

A directed graph is strongly connected if in the graph, any node is reachable from any other node by traversing edges following their directions. $(f + 1)$-strong connectivity and $n > f$ are together sufficient, because we are able to route messages between any pair of fault-free nodes even if up to f nodes crash, which can be used to implement the reliable broadcast primitive among fault-free nodes; thus, simulation of any crash-tolerant consensus algorithm in complete graphs is possible in such directed graphs. To see that $(f + 1)$-strong connectivity is not necessary, consider Figure 2.2. This network is *not* strongly connected; yet, when $f = 0$ (every node is fault-free), consensus is possible by having both nodes choose node v_1's input as output.

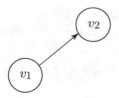

Figure 2.2: A network that is *not* strongly connected but still allows consensus.

Asymmetric Information Flow   These two generalizations are not adequate for specifying *tight* conditions on directed networks because they do not completely capture the notion of "asymmetric information flow." One way to capture such notion is by the usage of a "reduced graph" [86, 93, 98] as shown in the following claim.

Claim 2.1 *It is possible to achieve crash–tolerant consensus in synchronous systems in a graph G while tolerating up to f crash faults <u>if and only if</u> after removing up to f nodes and all the links incident to the removed nodes in G, there exists a* source *node that can reach other nodes in the remaining graph (reduced graph), i.e., there exists a directed rooted spanning tree in the reduced graph.*

In the claim, the "remaining graph" is the reduced graph for crash-tolerant consensus in synchronous systems [93]. Due to the existence of a directed rooted spanning tree in each reduced graph, information disseminated by at least one *source* node (specified in the claim) can be shared by all the fault-free nodes. Later, we discuss other forms of reduced graphs for other consensus problems. Note that for a given G and a given f, there may exist multiple reduced graphs. The condition requires that a directed rooted spanning tree exists in *all* possible reduced graphs. In the fault-free case ($f = 0$), the condition requires the existence of a directed rooted spanning tree in G. For example, the network in Figure 2.2 satisfies the condition, whereas the network in Figure 2.1 does not satisfy the condition for $f = 0$. Now, consider the example network in Figure 2.3. This network satisfies the condition in Claim 2.1 for $f = 1$, since after removing up to 1 node, the reduced graph is a directed rooted spanning tree.

It should be straightforward to observe that the condition in Claim 2.1 is necessary, since if there is no such spanning tree after removing up to f nodes, then we can find a failure pattern to "block" the flow of any shared information between some pair of fault-free nodes. It is less obvious why the condition is sufficient, since the spanning tree may change over time because some nodes crash. Later, we discuss a consensus algorithm from [93] that relies on the observation that no matter how the failures occur, there is a directed rooted spanning tree that can "propagate" the information. In the algorithm, each node does not know the structure of the spanning tree; however, the algorithm still ensures that *at some point of time*, enough information can be propagated to all the nodes that have not crashed yet, and each node can use this information to achieve consensus.

Observations similar to Claim 2.1 were first made in the context of fault-free consensus [12, 42] and also in the context of various versions of fault-tolerant consensus problems [20, 86, 93, 98]. The exact manner in which the source node is identified differs for the different problems because of different assumptions on faulty behaviors, system models, and problem specifications. In the rest of this chapter, we will formally introduce some basic graph notions to facilitate our study of the relation between topology and consensus feasibility.

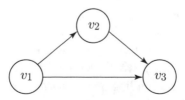

Figure 2.3: An example network that tolerates one crash fault.

2.3 NETWORK PRELIMINARIES

In this section we introduce some basic network terminology to facilitate the study of topological conditions inherently affecting consensus feasibility. Since most notions may refer to any graph, we will also refer to the corresponding processes of the communication graph simply as nodes.

2.3.1 THE NETWORK

We will consider a static, directed network of processes $G = (V, E)$, where V is the set of n processes (or nodes), and E is the set of directed edges between the processes in V. For ease of presentation we will also use the notations $V(G), E(G)$ for the node and edge sets respectively corresponding to graph G. We assume that $n \geq 2$, since the consensus problem variations we consider are trivial to solve for $n = 1$. A process i can transmit messages to another process j if directed edge (i, j) is in E. We also assume that each process can send messages to itself as well; however, for convenience, we exclude self-loops from set E. We will often use the terms *edge* and *link* interchangeably. Finally, all edges represent *reliable communication links*, defined below.

Definition 2.6 A *reliable communication link* has the following properties.

- Once a message is sent through the link, its content cannot be altered by the adversary in any way.

- The ID of the sender of the message is always known to the recipient. Moreover, all edges represent FIFO (first-in-first-out) channels and deliver each transmitted message exactly once.

2.3.2 GRAPH TERMINOLOGY

Upper case letters are used to name sets. Lower case italic letters are used to name processes. All paths used in our discussion are directed paths. Process j is said to be an incoming neighbor of process i if $(j, i) \in E$. Let N_i^- be the set of incoming neighbors of process i, i.e., $N_i^- = \{j \mid (j, i) \in E\}$. Define N_i^+ as the set of outgoing neighbors of process i, i.e., $N_i^+ = \{j \mid (i, j) \in E\}$. More generally, with $N_i(k)^-, N_i(k)^+$, we will denote the sets of k-hop incoming and outgoing neighbors of i, respectively. More specifically, a k-hop incoming (resp. outgoing) neighbor of i is a process j which is connected with i through a directed path of length at most k, starting from j and ending on i (resp. starting from i and ending on j). Since in undirected graphs the sets of incoming and outgoing neighbors of a process i coincide, in the results on undirected networks presented, we will omit the $+, -$ superscripts and simply denote the neighborhood of a process i with N_i.

For set $B \subseteq V$, process i is said to be an incoming neighbor of set B if $i \notin B$, and there exists $j \in B$ such that $(i, j) \in E$. Given subsets of nodes A and B, set B is said to have k incoming neighbors in set A if A contains k distinct incoming neighbors of B.

2.3.3 COMMUNICATION REDUNDANCY BETWEEN SETS

The existence of faulty processes might disrupt the communication between sets of fault-free processes. Therefore, in order to achieve more complex distributed tasks such as consensus, redundant communication between sets of processes is needed. Essentially, redundant communication links should appear in the network since some of them might fail to propagate the correct information due to corruptions. In the following, we present some fundamental notions, regarding the connectivity of process sets, which are important for the study of consensus in directed networks.

Definition 2.7   Given disjoint non-empty subsets of nodes A and B, we will say that $A \overset{x}{\rightarrowtail} B$ holds, if B has at least x distinct incoming neighbors in A. The negation of $A \overset{x}{\rightarrowtail} B$ will be denoted by $A \overset{x}{\not\rightarrowtail} B$.

Consider the network in Figure 2.4, which contains two cliques K_1 and K_2, each consisting of 7 nodes (Note that the edges within cliques K_1 and K_2 are not depicted). Within each clique, each node has a directed link to the other 6 nodes in that clique—these links within each clique are not shown in the figure. There are 8 directed links with one endpoint in clique K_1 and the other endpoint in clique K_2. In the network, K_2 has 4 incoming neighbors in K_1, namely u_1, u_2, u_3, and u_4. Thus, $K_1 \overset{4}{\rightarrowtail} K_2$. Similarly, $K_2 \overset{4}{\rightarrowtail} K_1$.

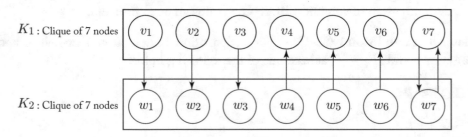

Figure 2.4: A network that illustrates redundant communication between sets.

Definition 2.8   Given disjoint non-empty subsets of nodes A and B, $A \overset{x}{\twoheadrightarrow} B$ if there exists a node in B that has at least x distinct incoming neighbors in A. The negation of $A \overset{x}{\twoheadrightarrow} B$ will be denoted by $A \overset{x}{\not\twoheadrightarrow} B$.

We next highlight the differences between notations $\twoheadrightarrow$ and $\rightarrowtail$. Notation $A \twoheadrightarrow B$ means that *there exists* a node in B that has enough incoming neighbors in A; whereas, $A \rightarrowtail B$ means that all nodes in B *jointly* have enough incoming neighbors that are in A. Notations $\rightarrowtail$ and $\twoheadrightarrow$ are used to specify conditions for general and iterative algorithms, respectively. In

Figure 2.4, $K_1 \overset{2}{\not\rightarrowtail} K_2$, since all nodes in set K_2 have at most one incoming neighbors from set K_1.

2.4   NETWORK TOPOLOGY AND CONSENSUS

We next summarize some topological conditions which prove to capture consensus feasibility in different models. The conditions were introduced in a series of works [86, 87, 93, 98] studying consensus variations under different assumptions. Recall that the problem formulations were introduced in Section 1.3.

2.4.1   GENERAL ALGORITHMS

First, we define the topological conditions pertinent to achieving several consensus variations via general algorithms. Note that, in this case, the notion $\rightarrowtail$ defined in Definition 2.7, proves to be appropriate for the specification of the tight conditions. We name the topological conditions presented in Definitions 2.9, 2.10 and 2.11 as **CCS-G** (abbreviating Crash-Consensus-Synchronous-General), **CCA-G** (Crash-Consensus-Asynchronous-General) and **BCS-G** (Byzantine-Consensus-Synchronous-General), respectively. The conditions prove to be necessary and sufficient for the respective settings as will be argued in the corresponding chapters. Characterization of the necessary and sufficient condition on the network topology for using general algorithms to solve approximate Byzantine consensus in asynchronous systems, i.e., determination of condition **BCA-G** remains an open problem.

Definition 2.9   (Condition CCS-G).   For any partition F, L, C, R of V, where L and R are both non-empty, and $|F| \leq f$, at least one of the following holds:

- $L \cup C \overset{1}{\rightarrowtail} R$
- $R \cup C \overset{1}{\rightarrowtail} L$

Definition 2.10   (Condition CCA-G).   For any partition L, C, R of V, where L and R are both non-empty, at least one of the following holds:

- $L \cup C \overset{f+1}{\rightarrowtail} R$
- $R \cup C \overset{f+1}{\rightarrowtail} L$

Definition 2.11   (Condition BCS-G).   For any partition F, L, C, R of V, where L and R are both non-empty, and $|F| \leq f$, at least one of the following holds:

- $L \cup C \overset{f+1}{\rightarrowtail} R$

- $R \cup C \overset{f+1}{\rightarrowtail} L$

The network shown in Figure 2.4 above satisfies Condition BCS-G for $f = 2$, whereas the network in Figure 2.3 above satisfies Condition CCS-G for $f = 1$. Note that the condition in Claim 2.1 is indeed equivalent to Condition CCS-G as will be discussed in the following.

2.4.2 ITERATIVE ALGORITHMS

Below, we list the results for solving different consensus problems using iterative algorithms. In this case, the notion $\twoheadrightarrow$ defined in Definition 2.8, proves to be appropriate for the specification of the tight conditions. We name the topological conditions presented in Definitions 2.12, 2.13, 2.14, and 2.15 as **CCS-I** (abbreviating Crash-Consensus-Synchronous-Iterative), **CCA-I** (Crash-Consensus-Asynchronous-Iterative), **BCS-I** (Byzantine-Consensus-Synchronous-Iterative), and **BCA-I** (Byzantine-Consensus-Asynchronous-Iterative), respectively. Similarly with the general algorithms case, these conditions prove to be necessary and sufficient for solving the respective consensus variations using iterative algorithms. Determination of the necessary and sufficient condition for solving exact Byzantine consensus with iterative algorithms in synchronous systems remains an open question. Note that Condition CCS-G is identical to Condition CCS-I; however, all the other conditions for synchronous and asynchronous systems are not equal to their counterparts.

Definition 2.12 (Condition CCS-I). For any partition F, L, C, R of V, where L and R are both non-empty, and $|F| \leq f$, at least one of the following holds:

- $L \cup C \overset{1}{\twoheadrightarrow} R$

- $R \cup C \overset{1}{\twoheadrightarrow} L$

Definition 2.13 (Condition CCA-I). For any partition L, C, R of V, where L and R are both non-empty, at least one of the following holds:

- $L \cup C \overset{f+1}{\twoheadrightarrow} R$

- $R \cup C \overset{f+1}{\twoheadrightarrow} L$

Definition 2.14 (Condition BCS-I). For any partition F, L, C, R of V, where L and R are both non-empty, and $|F| \leq f$, at least one of the following holds:

- $L \cup C \overset{f+1}{\twoheadrightarrow} R$

- $R \cup C \overset{f+1}{\twoheadrightarrow} L$

Definition 2.15 (Condition BCA-I). For any partition F, L, C, R of V, where L and R are both non-empty, and $|F| \leq f$, at least one of the following holds:

- $L \cup C \overset{2f+1}{\twoheadrightarrow} R$

- $R \cup C \overset{2f+1}{\twoheadrightarrow} L$

Note that in Condition CCA-G (Definition 2.10) and Condition CCA-I (Definition 2.13), the partition does not need set F, unlike other conditions.

Intuition   For consensus to be achieved, there must be a way for information to "flow between" different subsets of fault-free processes (subsets L and R in the theorems above), despite the presence of faulty processes (subset F). The different conditions above capture this intuition. Observe that, in each case, for different values of x, we obtain the requirement of the form "either $L \cup C \overset{x}{\twoheadrightarrow} R$ or $R \cup C \overset{x}{\twoheadrightarrow} L$" (or analogously $L \cup C \overset{x}{\twoheadrightarrow} R$ or $R \cup C \overset{x}{\twoheadrightarrow} L$). Intuitively, after removing the subset F (i.e., isolating the faulty behavior), information must be able to "flow" either from $L \cup C$ to R, or from $R \cup C$ to L in the remaining graph, but it is not necessary that the information flows in both directions—this "asymmetry" in the necessary and sufficient condition is a consequence of the directed nature of the communication network. The value of x is to ensure that some fault-free processes in either L or R have enough redundant information/messages to mask faulty behaviors.

For general algorithms, we use $\rightarrowtail$, because with the topology information and the ability to route message, processes in the set R or L may be able to share information within the set. In contrast, for iterative algorithms, computation is performed locally and, thus, we use $\twoheadrightarrow$ to represent the tight condition. That is, every process requires enough incoming neighbors from outside. Last, in many cases, we are able to obtain an equivalent condition that requires the existence of directed rooted spanning tree in the reduced graph. For example, the condition in Claim 2.1 is equivalent to Condition CCS-G (in Definition 2.9).[2]

2.5   RELATIONS AMONG TIGHT CONDITIONS

As noted above, the tight conditions presented capture how information can "flow between" different subsets of fault-free nodes despite the presence of faulty nodes under different synchrony

---

[2]As shown in [86, 93, 98], the manner of constructing reduced graphs varies for different consensus problems. Claim 2.1 only provides the construction for crash-tolerant consensus in synchronous systems.

assumptions. The relations between the conditions have been identified by Tseng and Vaidya in a series of works and can be found in [87]. We next present the relations summarized in the theorems, the proofs of which are presented in the corresponding chapters that each condition is studied.

Note on Condition relations   Observe that conditions defined in Definitions 2.9–2.15 are parameterized by the global adversary bound f. We stress out that whenever we state that Condition A implies Condition B (denoted $A \Rightarrow B$), it is implied that this holds for the same corruption bound-parameter f in both conditions. Another trivial fact to consider is that for parameters $f < f'$, $A_{f'} \Rightarrow A_f$ holds, where A_f denotes Condition A parameterized with value f.

The first two theorems below show that the conditions related to general algorithms (respectively iterative algorithms) can be totally ordered by the relation of strict implication.

Theorem 2.16   Relation of General Algorithms Conditions.

$$BCS\text{-}G \Rightarrow CCA\text{-}G \Rightarrow CCS\text{-}G$$

Moreover, no two of these conditions are equivalent.

Theorem 2.17   Relation of Iterative Algorithms Conditions.

$$BCA\text{-}I \Rightarrow BCS\text{-}I \Rightarrow CCA\text{-}I \Rightarrow CCS\text{-}I$$

Moreover, no two of these conditions are equivalent.

The following theorem shows the relations between the two groups of conditions related to general and iterative algorithms.

Theorem 2.18

- $CCS\text{-}I \Leftrightarrow CCS\text{-}G.$

- $CCA\text{-}I \Rightarrow CCA\text{-}G$ *and* $CCA\text{-}I \nLeftarrow CCA\text{-}G$

- $BCS\text{-}I \Rightarrow BCS\text{-}G$ *and* $BCS\text{-}I \nLeftarrow BCS\text{-}G$

The relations between the conditions are depicted in Figure 2.5 where set A represents the class of graphs for which Condition A holds.

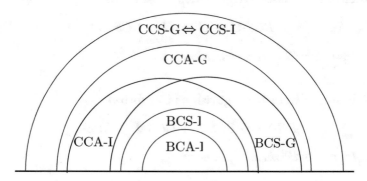

Figure 2.5: Relations of the tight topological conditions. All inclusions are strict.

PART II

Consensus with a Global Adversary

CHAPTER 3

Synchronous Crash Fault Tolerance

In this chapter, we consider crash-tolerant consensus in synchronous systems. We first discuss topological conditions that determine the feasibility of the problem beginning with conditions CCS-I and CCS-G (presented in Definitions 2.12 and 2.9 in Section 2.4, respectively). We show, by standard indistinguishability arguments, that not satisfaction of these conditions renders synchronous crash-tolerant consensus impossible. In other words, these conditions are necessary. In the last part of the chapter, we present a simple iterative algorithm that achieves approximate consensus followed by a variation of iterative algorithm that achieves exact consensus. Note that we consider a system of n processes, up to f of them may suffer crash failures; the remaining ones are assumed to correctly execute the protocol.

3.1 TOPOLOGICAL CONDITIONS AND IMPLICATIONS

In this section, we discuss the topological conditions associated with the solvability of synchronous crash-tolerant consensus, and their relation.

Theorem 3.1 *Conditions CCS-I and CCS-G are equivalent.*

Proof. Observe that by Definitions 2.7 and 2.8, for any process set A, B, the notions of $A \xrightarrow{x} B$ and $A \xrightarrow{x} B$ coincide for $x = 1$. The only difference in the definitions of conditions CCS-I and CCS-G (Definitions 2.12 and 2.9, respectively) is that the former uses the $\xrightarrow{x}$ relation while the latter uses the $\xrightarrow{x}$ relation. Consequently, for any process sets A, B, every occurrence of $A \xrightarrow{1} B$ in Definition 2.9, can be replaced with the equivalent expression $A \xrightarrow{1} B$, and this will make it identical to Definition 2.12. Thus, the conditions are identical by definition. $\square$

Next, we present another condition that is equivalent to CCS-I and CCS-G. The condition is more intuitive and allows for a concise proof for the sufficiency of conditions CCS-G and CCS-I.

For any $F \subseteq V$, we will denote with G_F the subgraph of G induced by the process set $V \setminus F$. We will use the following supplementary definitions.

Definition 3.2   Source Node of Graph.   For $G = (V, E)$, a node $s \in V$ is said to be a *source* if it is connected to every other node i in V via directed paths that initiate in s and end in i.

We next define the Condition CCS-Source (Crash-Consensus-Synchronous-Source).

Definition 3.3   Condition CCS-Source.   Condition CCS-Source holds in graph G if for any $F \subseteq V$, such that $|F| \leq f$, there exists at least one source node in G_F.

Another way to express Condition CCS-Source is that there exists a directed rooted spanning tree (i.e., an arborescence) in any induced graph G_F, which has the source node as the root.

Theorem 3.4   *Conditions CCS-I, CCS-G, and CCS-Source are equivalent.*

Proof.   Since conditions CCS-I and CCS-G have been proven equivalent in Theorem 3.1, in the following, we will just refer to Condition CCS-I. The proof of the theorem is by contradiction. Suppose that Graph $G = (V, E)$ satisfies Condition CCS-I, and for some $F \subseteq V$, $|F| \leq f$, there exists a pair of nodes $i, j \notin F$ such that there is no node s that has directed paths to both i and j in subgraph G_F induced by nodes in $V \setminus F$. For the subgraph G_F and a node x in $V \setminus F$, define S_x as the set of all nodes that have directed paths in G_F to node x. Note that S_x contains x as well, because x trivially has a path to itself.

By assumption, S_i and S_j are disjoint. Moreover, there must be no path from any node in S_i to any node in S_j in G_F, and vice versa, since otherwise, there would exist some node that can reach both nodes i and j, which contradicts our assumption above. Now, define L, C, R as follows:

- $L := S_i$

- $R := S_j$

- $C := V \setminus (F \cup L \cup R)$

Then, we make the following observations:

- *F and C may be empty, but L and R are non-empty*: this is true because $i \in S_i = L$ and $j \in S_j = R$.

- *Nodes in C (if non-empty) have no link to nodes in $L \cup R$*: if some nodes $c \in C$ has a link to some node $x \in L = S_i$, then c will be able to reach node i on a directed path via node x (since $x \in S_i$ has a path to i, by definition of set S_i). This would then imply that c must be in S_i, however, that contradicts the definition of C as $V \setminus (F \cup L \cup R)$. By a similar argument, nodes in C cannot have links to nodes in R.

- *There is no link from any node in L to nodes in R, and vice versa*: Recall that $L = S_i$ and $R = S_j$. If some node $x \in L$ has a link to a node $y \in R$, then x will have a directed path to node j via node y. However, this contradicts our assumption above that no node has directed paths to both i and j.

These observations together imply that $L \cup C \overset{1}{\not\twoheadrightarrow} R$ and $C \cup R \overset{1}{\not\twoheadrightarrow} L$. That is, $G = (V, E)$ does not satisfy Condition CCS-I. This is a contradiction. Thus, CCS-I implies CCS-Source.

Conversely, we next show that CCS-Source implies CCS-I. Assume that CCS-I does not hold, then there exists a partition of V in sets F, L, C, R with $|F| \leq f, L, R \neq \emptyset$ such that both the following hold:

$$L \cup C \overset{1}{\not\twoheadrightarrow} R \tag{1}$$

$$R \cup C \overset{1}{\not\twoheadrightarrow} L \tag{2}$$

Since $L, R \neq \emptyset$ let, $i \in L$ and $j \in R$. Observe that (1) implies that no node in L is connected by a directed path to j. Similarly, (2) implies that no node in R is connected by a directed path to i. Moreover, even if $C \neq \emptyset$, (1),(2) imply that no node in C is connected by a directed path to i or j. Consequently, there is no source node for induced subgraph G_F and thus CCS-Source does not hold. $\qquad\square$

As argued before, the theorem shows the existence of a directed rooted spanning tree in all induced graphs G_F, which has the source node as the root. Presence of such "source" node (or root) is crucial in achieving consensus. Similar observations were first made in the context of fault-free consensus [12, 42], and also in the context of other versions of fault-tolerant consensus problems [13, 19, 94, 98] (although the exact manner in which the source node is identified differs for the different problems).

3.2   NECESSITY OF CONDITIONS CCS-I AND CCS-G

It is straightforward why these conditions are necessary, since to achieve consensus, some shared information needs to "flow" between any two subsets of fault-free processes after some other processes crash. If the conditions do not hold for the graph G, then it is possible to find a subset of up to f processes whose removal would "block" the flow of shared information between two sets of remaining processes. For completeness, we present the necessity proof for CCS-G below, i.e., if G does not satisfy Condition CCS-G, then it is impossible to achieve approximate or exact consensus if up to f processes may fail. The proof is adapted from the one in [93]. Since CCS-I is identical to CCS-G and iterative algorithms are a subclass of general algorithms, the proof also applies to Condition CCS-I.

All the necessity proofs presented in this book have a similar structure.

- Identify a set of processes F to be faulty processes.

- Show that under a specific input distribution, and a certain faulty behavior of processes in F will make the fault-free processes, processes in $V \setminus F$, unable to obtain a correct output.

The second part is based on the indistinguishability argument [58], which shows that either validity or agreement would be violated. Due to different model assumptions, there are some differences in the proof details.

NECESSITY PROOF OF CONDITION CCS-G

Proof. The proof is by contradiction. Suppose that there exists a consensus algorithm $\mathcal{A}$ for graph $G = (V, E)$, but G does not satisfy Condition CCS-G. In other words, there exists a partition of processes F, L, C, R of V such that

- $|F| \leq f$;

- L and R are both non-empty; and

- $L \cup C \overset{1}{\nrightarrow} R$ and $R \cup C \overset{1}{\nrightarrow} L$.

The last two assumptions imply that processes in $L \cup C$ have no links to processes in R, and processes in $R \cup C$ have no links to processes in L.

Now, consider an execution of the consensus algorithm $\mathcal{A}$ where F is the set of faulty processes. Moreover, all the processes in F crash before the start of the algorithm $\mathcal{A}$. All the other processes are assumed to be fault-free in the execution. Such an execution is possible, since by assumption, $|F| \leq f$. Also, suppose that all the processes in L have input 0, and all the processes in R have input 1. Nodes in C may have input either 0 or 1.

Consider any process $x \in L$. Since processes in F crash before taking any steps in the algorithm $\mathcal{A}$, and as noted above, there are no links from $C \cup R$ to any process in L, the only input value that could be possibly learned by x throughout the execution of the algorithm $\mathcal{A}$ is 0. Then to satisfy the validity property, 0 must be the output of process x.

Similarly, any process y in R can only learn input values 1 throughout the execution of the algorithm $\mathcal{A}$, and thus, 1 must be the output of process y. Since L and R are non-empty and consist of fault-free processes, the above observations imply that the agreement property is violated. This is a contradiction. □

3.3   APPROXIMATE CONSENSUS ALGORITHM

In this section, we present Algorithm *Average* (pseudo-code in Algorithm 3.1), a synchronous IAC algorithm as defined in Section 1.4.1. It is a simple adaption of algorithms that were studied extensively in the literature of both fault tolerance and control theory, e.g., [28, 53]. What differentiates this type of algorithms from others used for incomplete network consensus is that each process does *not* act as a relayer and thus does *not* forward any message. Instead, processes update their local state values after the end of each iteration in prior algorithms. For consistency of the presentation and the proofs, we present an adapted algorithm in Algorithm 3.1 in which processes need to forward messages. For simplicity, we assume that the input at each process is some *real number* in the range $[0, K]$, where $K \in \mathbb{R}$ is known *a priori*.

Note that if $K < \epsilon$, then the problem is trivial, so K is assumed to be $\geq \epsilon$. The existence of this bound can be easily shown to guarantee the termination requirement of the algorithms presented in this chapter (cf., Theorem 3.6). However, the assumption can be dropped and the termination property can be shown to hold in the same way it holds for analogous algorithms presented in [28, 44, 58].

Algorithm 3.1 *Average*

(For process $i \in V$)
Initialization: $v_i[0] :=$ input of node i
Constant: $p_{end} > \log_{n/(n-1)} \frac{K}{\epsilon}$

1: **for** round $t := 1$ to p_{end} **do**
2:    $S_i := \{(i, v_i[t-1])\}$
3:    **for** n iterations **do**
4:        Send S_i to all the processes in $N_i^+ \cup \{i\}$
5:        Receive values from $N_i^- \cup \{i\}$ and create set $S_i[t]$
6:        $S_i := S_i \cup S_i[t]$ ▷ $S_i[t]$ Denotes the set of values received in the previous step
7:    **end for**
8:    $v_i[t] := \text{average}(\{v \mid (j, v) \in S_i\})$ ▷ update local state
9: **end for**
10: **output** $v_i[t]$

Note that S_i is *not* a multi-set, as process ID is assumed to be unique. Moreover, for brevity, Algorithm *Average* does not optimize the message and space complexity. For example, each process i does not need to transmit whole S_i, and it only needs to maintain a single state variable. The current presentation allows us to prove the correctness more compactly.

Correctness of Algorithm Average

In a given execution of Algorithm *Average*, denote by $F[p]$ the set of crashed processes by the end of phase p. By definition, each process in $V \setminus F[p]$ successfully updates its local state at the end of phase p. For each pair of processes $i, j \in V \setminus F[p]$, let V_i and V_j denote the set that i

and j used to update its value, respectively. We first begin with an important observation on V_i and V_j.

Lemma 3.5   *If $G = (V, E)$ satisfies Condition CCS-G (or equivalently CCS-I), then there is a common value in V_i and V_j. In other words, $V_i \cap V_j \neq \emptyset$.*

Proof. By Theorem 3.4 and the assumption that G satisfies Condition CCS-G, processes in $V \setminus F[p]$ must have a source node $s \in V \setminus F[p]$ that can reach every other process in $G_{F[p]}$. Recall that $G_{F[p]}$ is a subgraph induced by nodes in $V \setminus F[p]$. Since each process sends and forwards messages for n iteration in phase p, each process in $V \setminus F[p]$ must receive a message from process s which contains its state value $v_s[p-1]$. This proves the lemma. $\square$

Validity of Algorithm *Average* is obvious, since we only consider crash faults, and each process uses the average function to update its local state. Now, we prove that the algorithm also satisfies the convergence property.

Theorem 3.6   *Algorithm Average satisfies the ϵ-agreement and termination properties.*

Proof. For $p \geq 1$, define

$$M[p] = \max_{i \in V \setminus F[p]} v_i[p] \tag{3.1}$$

and

$$m[p] = \min_{i \in V \setminus F[p]} v_i[p]. \tag{3.2}$$

With a slight abuse of terminology, let $M[0]$ and $m[0]$ denote the upper bound and the lower bound on the input values, respectively. Recall that we have assumed that the input range is $[0, K]$, where $K \geq \epsilon$. Thus,

$$M[0] = K \quad \text{and} \quad m[0] = 0.$$

Recall that $F[t]$ denote the set of crashed processes by the end of iteration t. Then, define $\psi[t]$ as the maximum difference between states at processes in $V \setminus F[t]$ in the end of iteration t. In other words,

$$\psi[t] = M[t] - m[t]. \tag{3.3}$$

Denote by $\|x\|$ the absolute value of a real number x. Then, we have

$$\psi[t] = \max_{i,j \in V \setminus F[t]} \|v_i[t] - v_j[t]\|. \tag{3.4}$$

By definition of $m[t-1]$ and $M[t-1]$, for each process $k \in V \setminus F[p-1]$, we have

$$m[t-1] \leq v_k[t-1] \leq M[t-1] \tag{3.5}$$

$$m[t-1] \le v_k[t-1] \le M[t-1]. \tag{3.6}$$

Now consider a pair of processes $i, j \in V \setminus F[p]$. Let $s_i = |V_i|$, the size of V_i. Similarly, let $s_i = |V_j|$. By Lemma 3.5, there exists a common value in V_i and V_j. Denote by c the common value in the sets. Note that by assumption c is a state of some process in $V \setminus F[t-1]$. Thus, $m[t-1] \le c \le M[t-1]$. Define

$$\gamma = \frac{1}{n}.$$

By assumption, we have

$$
\begin{aligned}
v_i[p] &= \sum_{v \in V_i} \frac{v}{s_i} v_k[p-1] \\
&\le \frac{c}{s_i} + (1 - \frac{1}{s_i})M[p-1] \quad \text{due to (3.1)} \\
&\le \gamma c + (\frac{1}{s_i} - \gamma)c + (1 - \frac{1}{s_i})M[p-1] \\
&\le \gamma c + (1-\gamma)M[p-1].
\end{aligned}
\tag{3.7}
$$

The last inequality is because $\gamma \le \frac{1}{s_i}$ and $c \le M[p-1]$.
Similarly, we have

$$
\begin{aligned}
v_j[p] &= \sum_{v \in V_j} \frac{1}{s_j} v_k[p-1] \\
&\ge \frac{c}{s_j} + (1 - \frac{1}{s_j})m[p-1] \quad \text{due to (3.2)} \\
&\ge \gamma c + (\frac{1}{r_j} - \gamma)c + (1 - \frac{1}{s_j})m[p-1] \\
&\ge \gamma c + (1-\gamma)m[p-1].
\end{aligned}
\tag{3.8}
$$

The last inequality is because $\gamma \le \frac{1}{s_j}$ and $c \ge m[p-1]$.
Now, subtracting (3.8) from (3.7), we get

$$v_i[p] - v_j[p] \le (1-\gamma)(M[p-1] - m[p-1]). \tag{3.9}$$

By swapping the role of i and j above, we can show that

$$v_j[p] - v_i[p] \le (1-\gamma)(M[p-1] - m[p-1]). \tag{3.10}$$

Equations (3.9) and (3.10) together imply that

$$
\begin{aligned}
\|v_i[p] - v_j[p]\| &\le (1-\gamma)(M[p-1] - m[p-1]) \\
&\le (1-\gamma)\psi[p-1] \quad \text{due to \ (3.3).}
\end{aligned}
$$

The first inequality is because $M[p-1] \geq m[p-1]$. The above inequality holds for each pair of processes i, j that have computed $v[p]$ in phase p, so we have

$$\max_{i,j \in V \setminus F[p]} \|v_i[p] - v_j[p]\| \leq (1-\gamma)\psi[p-1].$$

This together with Equation (3.4) imply that

$$M[p] - m[p] \leq (1-\gamma)(M[p-1] - m[p-1]). \tag{3.11}$$

By repeated application of (3.11), we get

$$M[p] - m[p] \leq (1-\gamma)^p (M[0] - m[0]). \tag{3.12}$$

Therefore, for a given $\epsilon > 0$, if

$$p > \log_{1/(1-\gamma)} \frac{M[0] - m[0]}{\epsilon}, \tag{3.13}$$

then

$$M[p] - m[p] < \epsilon. \tag{3.14}$$

Recall that we have assumed that the input range is $[0, K]$. Also, $\gamma = \frac{1}{n}$. Then, if we choose

$$p_{end} > \log_{n/(n-1)} \frac{K}{\epsilon},$$

then the algorithm satisfies ϵ-agreement property due to (3.13) and (3.14). $\square$

3.4   EXACT CONSENSUS ALGORITHM

In this section, we present Algorithm Min-Max, which was first proposed in [93], and was proved to achieve binary consensus. The algorithm was first proved to achieve multivalued consensus in [21]. In [93], the authors did not realize that Algorithm Min-Max actually achieves multi-valued consensus, and proposed another algorithm, Algorithm MVC (Multi-Valued-Consensus) which is less efficient and can only deal with integer inputs. We stress that Algorithm 3.2 dominates the Average algorithm both in terms of convergence time (or round complexity) and accuracy. The benefit of the Average algorithm is that it belongs in the specific class of IAC algorithms, which offer some advantages discussed in Section 1.4.3.

3.4.1   ALGORITHM MIN-MAX

To achieve consensus, each process i performs Algorithm *Min-Max* passing its input value as the parameter to Algorithm *Min-Max*. Algorithm Min-Max uses *Compute* as a sub-routine. *Compute* has two parameters: t, which is i's local state, and *Function*, which may be specified as *min* and *max*. In the last step of each round in *Compute* at process i, the *Function* is applied to set S_i. $\min(S_i)$ returns the minimum of the values in set S_i, and $\max(S_i)$ returns the maximum of the values in set S_i.

Algorithm 3.2 Min-Max

(For process $i \in V$)

Initialization: $v_i[0] :=$ input of node i

1: **for** phase number $p := 1$ to $2f + 2$ **do**
2:     **if** $p \bmod 2 = 0$ **then**   ▷ **Min Phase**
3:         $v_i[p] :=$ Compute $(v_i[p-1], min)$
4:     **else**   ▷ **Max Phase**
5:         $v_i[p] :=$ Compute$(v_i[p-1], max)$
6:     **end if**
7: **end for**
8: **return** $v_i[2f + 2]$

Algorithm 3.3 Compute(t, *Function*)

(For process $i \in V$)

Initialization: $\tau_i := t$

1: **for** round $t := 1$ to n **do**
2:     Send τ_i to all the processes in $N_i^+ \cup \{i\}$
3:     Receive values from $N_i^- \cup \{i\}$ and create set S_i
4:     $\tau_i := Function(S_i)$ ▷ S_i denotes the set of values received in the previous step
5: **end for**
6: **return** τ_i

3.4.2 CORRECTNESS OF ALGORITHM MIN-MAX

Now, we are ready to show the correctness of Algorithm Min-Max. The proof of correctness assumes that graph $G = (V, E)$ satisfies Condition CCS-G and hence Condition CCS-Source. The proof is adapted from [21].

Theorem 3.7 *Algorithm Min-Max satisfies the termination, agreement, and validity properties.*

Proof. Since Algorithm Min-Max executes a fixed number of phases, its termination occurs in finite time. Validity is satisfied trivially as well. Now we prove that the algorithm satisfies the agreement property. We start by observing that *Compute*(t, min) never returns a value larger than parameter t passed to *Compute*, and *Compute*(t, max) never returns a value smaller than parameter t passed to *Compute*.

Fix an execution of the algorithm. Since there are $2f + 2$ phases, there must exist a pair of consecutive phases p^*, $p^* + 1$ such that *no process crashes* in phases p^* and $p^* + 1$. Without loss of generality, let p^* be the Min Phase (i.e., $p^* \bmod 2 = 0$) and $p^* + 1$ be the Max Phase. Denote by F the set of processes that crash before starting phase p^*.

Theorem 3.4 implies the existence of a source process that has directed paths in G_F to all processes in $V \setminus F$. In general, there may be multiple such source nodes in G_F; we denote this set of sources by S. Assume that the minimum value of all sources in round $p^* - 1$ is

$$\min_{i \in S} v_i[p^* - 1] = m. \tag{1}$$

We consider the two cases below. In each case, we show that agreement is achieved.

- *Case I: For all fault-free nodes $i \in V \setminus F, v_i[p^* - 1] \geq m$.*
  Thus, during the Min Phase p^*, any process s will call *Compute*(m, min). Then during the first round of *Compute* in phase p^*, those processes in $V \setminus F$ with incoming links from process s will update their τ variable (within *Compute*) to be m because this is the minimum value by assumption, and all the processes receive it from all sources. Since a source node has directed paths (of length at most $n - 1$) to all the processes in G_F, it follows by induction that each process i in $V \setminus F$ will update its state τ_i to be m by the end of the $n - 1$ rounds performed within *Compute*. Thus, when *Compute* returns, $v_i[p^*]$ at each $i \in V \setminus F$ will be set to m. It is easy to see that the remaining phases will not change the value of v_i at the fault-free processes, ensuring agreement when the algorithm terminates.

- *Case II: There exists a non-empty set of processes $A \subseteq V \setminus (F \cup S)$ such that, for all processes $i \in A, v_i[p^* - 1] < m$.*
  We first argue that $\max_{i \in V \setminus F} v_i[p^*] = m$. Since m is the minimum state value over all sources in phase $p^* - 1$, all nodes $i \in V \setminus F$ will update their p^* state to $v_i[p^*]m' \leq m$. Also, all sources in $s \in S$ will update to $v_i[p^*] = m$. The latter holds because if there exists a source s that decides on $v_s[p^*] = m' > m$ that means that it had received value m' from a process i and thus $v_i[p^* - 1] = m' < m$. The latter can only occur if there is a directed path from i to s. But this implies that $i \in S$ with $v_i[p^* - 1] = m' < m$; a contradiction to (1). This shows that $\max_{i \in V \setminus F} v_i[p^*] = m$ and all sources $s \in S$ have $v_i[p^*] = m$.

  Next, we consider Max phase $p^* + 1$. All sources $s \in S$ have $v_i[p^*] = m$ and no processes crash during phase $p^* + 1$. Since $\max_{i \in V \setminus F} v_i[p^*] = m$, by an argument analogous to that used for Min Phase p^* in Case I above, it follows that, for all $i \in V \setminus F$, $v_i[p^* + 1] = m$, achieving agreement. Any additional phases beyond phase $p^* + 1$ will not result in violation of the agreement, similar to Case I.

$\square$

CHAPTER 4

Asynchronous Crash Fault Tolerance

In this chapter, we consider asynchronous systems under the existence of crash faults. Since exact consensus is impossible in this setting by [31], we only consider the approximate consensus problem and show the tightness of Conditions CCA-I and CCA-G for the classes of iterative and general algorithms, respectively. For simplicity, we assume that the input at each process is some *real number* in the range $[0, K]$, where $K \in \mathbb{R}$ is known *a priori*. Note that if $K < \epsilon$, then the problem is trivial, so K is assumed to be $\geq \epsilon$. The existence of this bound can be easily shown to guarantee the termination requirement of the algorithms presented in this chapter (e.g., Theorems 4.9 and 4.13). However, the assumption can be dropped and the termination property can be shown to hold in the same way it holds for analogous algorithms presented in [28, 44, 58].

4.1 CONDITIONS RELATIONS AND IMPLICATIONS

As shown below, Conditions CCA-I, and CCA-G both imply a lower bound of $2f + 1$ on the overall number of processes. Recall that there exist $|V| = n$ processes in the system, and at most f of which might be corrupted. The lower bounds implied by the aforementioned conditions are well-known results in complete and undirected graphs, e.g., [6, 58]. However, the implication shows that the conditions strictly generalize the known bounds in the case of directed incomplete networks. We summarize the bounds in the theorem presented below.

Theorem 4.1

1. *Condition CCA-I implies that $n \geq 2f + 1$.*

2. *Condition CCA-G implies that $n \geq 2f + 1$.*

Proof.

(1) For $f = 0$, the claim is trivially true, since we assume that $n \geq 2$. Now consider $f > 0$; the proof is by contradiction. Suppose that $n \leq 2f$. Partition V into three subsets L, R, F such that $F = \emptyset, 0 < |L| \leq f$, and $0 < |R| \leq f$. Such a partition can be found because $2 \leq n \leq 2f$.

Since L, R are both non-empty, and contain at most f nodes each, we have $L \cup C \overset{f+1}{\nrightarrow} R$ and $R \cup C \overset{f+1}{\nrightarrow} L$, violating Condition CCA-I. This proves the claim.

(2) can be proved similarly. □

The next theorem shows the relation between the Conditions CCA-I, CCA-G studied in this chapter and Conditions CCS-I, CCS-G studied in Chapter 3.

Theorem 4.2

1. *CCA-I strictly implies CCA-G.*

2. *CCA-I strictly implies CCS-I.*

3. *CCA-G strictly implies CCS-G.*

Proof.

1. By definition it holds that for any sets of nodes A, B, $A \overset{f+1}{\rightarrow} B$ implies $A \overset{f+1}{\rightarrowtail} B$. Since this is the only difference in the definition of Conditions CCA-I, CCA-G, it follows that CCA-I implies CCA-G.

   To see that the conditions are not equivalent, consider Figure 2.4 for $f = 3$. It can be shown that in this network CCA-G is satisfied since $K_1 \overset{4}{\rightarrowtail} K_2$ and $K_2 \overset{4}{\rightarrowtail} K_1$ hold. On the other hand, Condition CCA-I is not satisfied in this network for $L = K_1, R = K_2, C = \emptyset$.

2. We will prove that CCA-I implies CCS-I by contradiction. Suppose that graph G does not satisfy Condition CCS-I, i.e., there exists a node partition F, L, C, R of V such that $L \cup C \overset{1}{\nrightarrow} R$ and $R \cup C \overset{1}{\nrightarrow} L$. Then, define $C' = C \cup F$. Due to the fact that $|F| \leq f$, $L \cup C' \overset{f+1}{\nrightarrow} R$ and $R \cup C' \overset{f+1}{\nrightarrow} L$, violating Condition CCA-I. This proves that CCA-I implies CCS-I.

   Consider the example network in Figure 2.3. It is easy to see that this network satisfies Condition CCS-I; however, it does not satisfy Condition CCA-I when $L = \{v_1\}, C = \emptyset$ and $R = \{v_2, v_3\}$. Thus, CCS-I does not imply CCA-I.

3. We will prove that CCA-G implies CCS-G by contradiction. Suppose that graph G does not satisfy Condition CCS-G, i.e., there exists a node partition F, L, C, R of V such that $L \cup C \overset{1}{\nrightarrowtail} R$ and $R \cup C \overset{1}{\nrightarrowtail} L$. Then, define $C' = C \cup F$. Due to the fact that $|F| \leq f$,

$L \cup C' \overset{f+1}{\not\to} R$ and $R \cup C' \overset{f+1}{\not\to} L$, violating Condition CCA-G. This proves that CCA-G implies CCS-G.

Consider the example network in Figure 2.3. This network tolerates 1 crash fault in synchronous systems, since it satisfies Condition CCS-G; however, it does not satisfy Condition CCA-G when $L = \{v_1\}$, $C = \emptyset$ and $R = \{v_2, v_3\}$. Thus, CCS does not imply CCA.

□

4.2   ITERATIVE APPROXIMATE CONSENSUS

In this section, we analyze the feasibility of approximate consensus in the specific class of Iterative Approximate Consensus algorithms (IAC). As in the previous section, we consider asynchronous systems, and thus we will focus on the class of asynchronous IAC algorithms as defined in Section 1.4.2. As argued before, IAC algorithms are of specific interest because of their low requirements in terms of memory and amount of message relays. Note that asynchronous IAC algorithms differ from synchronous IAC algorithms in the following two points.

- The messages containing states are tagged by the phase index to which the states correspond.

- Each process i waits to receive only a certain number of messages m before updating its state.

As in the previous section, state $v_i[p]$ denotes the p-th update of the state of process i; this happens at the end of the p-th phase of the asynchronous algorithm ($p \geq 0$). Moreover, $v_i[0]$ denotes the initial state of i, i.e., the input at process i. Due to the asynchrony assumption, different processes may potentially perform their p-th phase at very different real times.

Considering the structure of asynchronous IAC presented in Section 1.4.2, observe that the end of the *Receive* step of a process is dictated by the reception of a certain number of messages m; after that the process proceeds with updating its state. For asynchronous IAC algorithms, we will use the following condition for the *Receive* step, which is a "local" version of the WAIT condition used in the WA algorithm presented in Section 4.3.2. The condition will be denoted by 1-WAIT denoting that a process will wait for messages from its 1-hop neighbors[1] and essentially defines the number m of awaited messages.

Receive step (Condition 1-WAIT)   Wait until the first $|N_i^-| - f$ messages tagged by index $t - 1$ are received on the incoming edges, breaking ties arbitrarily.

---

[1]In Section 6.2.2 we will present the generalization of this condition for k-hop incoming neighbors, named k-WAIT.

4.2.1 NECESSITY OF CONDITION CCA-I

The necessity proof is similar to the necessity proof of Condition CCA presented in Section 4.3.1 but specifically takes into consideration the locality of condition CCA-I.

Theorem 4.3 *If graph $G = (V, E)$ does not satisfy Condition CCA-I, then no IAC algorithm can achieve asynchronous approximate consensus in G.*

Proof. The proof is by contradiction. Suppose that there exists an iterative one-hop algorithm $\mathcal{A}$ which achieves asynchronous approximate consensus in $G = (V, E)$, and G does not satisfy Condition CCA-I. That is, there exists a node partition L, C, R such that L, R are non-empty, $L \cup C \overset{f+1}{\nrightarrow} R$ and $R \cup C \overset{f+1}{\nrightarrow} L$.

Let $O(L)$ denote the set of nodes $C \cup R$ that have outgoing links to nodes in L, i.e., $O(L) = \{i \mid i \in C \cup R, N_i^+ \cap L \neq \emptyset\}$. Similarly, define $O(R) = \{i \mid i \in C \cup L, N_i^+ \cap R \neq \emptyset\}$. Since $L \cup C \overset{f+1}{\nrightarrow} R$ and $R \cup C \overset{f+1}{\nrightarrow} L$, we have that for every $i \in L$, $|N_i^- \cap O(L)| \leq f$ and for every $i \in R$, $|N_i^- \cap O(R)| \leq f$.

Consider a scenario where (i) each node in L has input 0; (ii) each node in R has input ϵ; (iii) nodes in C (if non- empty) have arbitrary inputs in $[0, \epsilon]$; (iv) no node crashes; and (v) the message delay for communications channels from $O(L)$ to L and from $O(R)$ to R is arbitrarily large compared to all the other channels.

Consider nodes in L. Since messages from the set $O(L)$ take arbitrarily long to arrive at the nodes in L, and for every $i \in L$, $N_i^- \cap O(L) \leq f$, from the perspective of node i, its incoming neighbors in $O(L)$ appear to have crashed. The latter yields from the fact that algorithm $\mathcal{A}$ is one-hop, i.e., the case that for every $i, j \in L$, $N_i^- \cap O(L) = N_i^- \cap O(L) \leq f$ cannot be excluded by the messages exchanged in L and thus there is a case where all their neighbors in $O(L)$ are crashed. Thus, nodes in L must decide on their output without waiting to hear from the nodes in $O(L)$. Consequently, to satisfy the validity property, the output at each node in L has to be 0, since 0 is the input of all the nodes in L. Similarly, nodes in R must decide their output without hearing from the nodes in $O(R)$; they must choose output as ϵ, because the input at all the nodes in R is ϵ. Thus, the ϵ-agreement property is violated, since the difference between outputs at fault-free nodes is not $< \epsilon$. This is a contradiction. $\square$

4.2.2 SUFFICIENCY OF CONDITION CCA-I

For sufficiency, we present Algorithm 4.4 LocWA (Local-Wait-Average) below, which is essentially a local version of algorithm WA, presented in Section 4.3.2, and utilizes only one-hop information. Recall that by definition, no message relay takes place. In Algorithm LocWA, each process i maintains the set $heard_i[p]$ of immediate incoming neighbors from which i has received values during phase p. Each node i performs the averaging operation to update its state value when Condition 1-WAIT below holds for the first time in phase p.

Definition 4.4 Condition 1-WAIT. The condition is satisfied at node i, in phase p, when $|heard_i[p]| \geq |N_i^-| - f$, i.e., when i has not received values from a set of at most f incoming neighbors.

Note that in the pseudo-code in Algorithm 4.4, lines 5–10 correspond to the receive step in asynchronous IAC algorithm (defined in Section 1.4.2).

Algorithm 4.4 LocWA (Local-Wait-Average)

(For process $i \in V$)
Initialization: $v_i[0] :=$ input at process i
Constant: p_{end} (Defined in 4.2.2)

1: **for** phase $p := 1$ **to** p_{end} **do**
2:     $R_i[p] := \{v_i[p-1]\}$
3:     $heard_i[p] := \{i\}$
4:     Send message $(v_i[p-1], i, p)$ to all the outgoing neighbors
5:     **repeat**
6:         **if** message (h, j, p) is received **then**
7:             $R_i[p] := R_i[p] \cup \{h\}$ $\triangleright$ $R_i[p]$ is a multiset
8:             $heard_i[p] := heard_i[p] \cup \{j\}$
9:         **end if**
10:     **until** Condition 1-WAIT is satisfied
11:     Update state as:

$$v_i[p] := \frac{\sum_{v \in R_i[p]} v}{|R_i[p]|} \tag{4.1}$$

12: **end for**
13: **output** $v_i[p]$

Number of phases p_{end} To argue about the termination of LocWA, in the following, we assume that p_{end} is any integer with

$$p_{end} > \frac{(n-f-1)\log(\epsilon/K)}{\log\left(1 - \frac{\alpha^{n-f-1}}{2}\right)},$$

where $\alpha = \min_{i \in V} \frac{1}{|N_i^-|}$. In the proof of Theorem 4.9, we show that this is sufficient to guarantee correct convergence of the algorithm.

Correctness Proof   Before presenting the proof (adapted from [84]), we present some useful definitions to facilitate the discussion.

Definition 4.5   For disjoint sets $A, B, in(A \to B)$ denotes the set of all the nodes in B that each have at least $f + 1$ incoming edges from nodes in A. When $A \not\to B$, define $in(A \to B) = \emptyset$. Formally, $in(A \to B) = \{ v \mid v \in B \text{ and } f + 1 \leq |N_v^- \cap A| \}$.

Definition 4.6   For *non-empty disjoint* sets A and B, set A is said to *propagate to* set B in l steps, where $l > 0$, if there exist sequences of sets $A_0, A_1, A_2, \cdots, A_l$ and $B_0, B_1, B_2, \cdots, B_l$ (propagating sequences) such that

- $A_0 = A, \quad B_0 = B, \quad A_l = A \cup B, \quad B_l = \emptyset, \quad B_\tau \neq \emptyset \text{ for } \tau < l \quad$ and

- for $0 \leq \tau \leq l - 1$, (i) $A_\tau \to B_\tau$; (ii) $A_{\tau+1} = A_\tau \cup in(A_\tau \to B_\tau)$; and (iii) $B_{\tau+1} = B_\tau - in(A_\tau \to B_\tau)$.

Observe that A_τ and B_τ form a partition of $A \cup B$, and for $\tau < l, in(A_\tau \to B_\tau) \neq \emptyset$. We say that set A propagates to set B if there is a propagating sequence for some steps l as defined above. Note that the number of steps l in the above definition is upper bounded by $n - f - 1$, since set A must be of size at least $f + 1$ for it to propagate to B; otherwise, $A \not\to B$.

Now, we present two key lemmas whose proofs are presented in [85]. In the discussion below, we assume that G satisfies Condition CCA-I.

Lemma 4.7   *For any partition A, B of V, where A, B are both non-empty, either A propagates to B, or B propagates to A.*

The lemma below states that the interval to which the states at all the fault-free nodes are confined shrinks after a finite number of phases of Algorithm LocWA. Recall that $M[p]$ and $m[p]$ denote the maximum and minimum states at the fault-free nodes at the end of the p-th phase.

Lemma 4.8   *Suppose that at the end of the p-th phase of Algorithm LocWA, V can be partitioned into non-empty sets R and L such that (i) R propagates to L in l steps, and (ii) the states of fault-free nodes in $R - F[p]$ are confined to an interval of length $\leq \frac{M[p]-m[p]}{2}$. Then, with Algorithm LocWA,*

$$M[p + l] - m[p + l] \leq \left(1 - \frac{\alpha^l}{2}\right)(m[p] - m[p]), \quad \text{where } \alpha = \min_{i \in V} \frac{1}{|N_i^-|}. \quad (4.2)$$

Using Lemma 4.8, we can prove the following theorem. Generally speaking, the proof proceeds as following: (i) nodes are divided into two disjoint sets, say L and R so that nodes have "closer" state values in each set; (ii) because each node receives an adequate set of messages, we show that under any delay and crash scenarios, at least one non-crashed node in either L or R will receive one message from the other set of nodes in each phase; and (iii) after enough phases, the value of all non-crashed nodes in either L or R will move "closer" to the values in the other set.

Theorem 4.9   *If $G = (V, E)$ satisfies Condition CCA-I, then Algorithm LocWA satisfies the validity, ϵ-agreement and termination properties.*

Proof. Validity is trivially true due to how Algorithm LocWA updates each node's state. Recall that $F[p]$ is defined as the processes that have *not* computed value $v[p]$ in phase p, i.e., processes in $F[p]$ have crashed before computing $v[p]$. Thus, $V \setminus F[p]$ is the set of processes that complete the computation of $v[p]$.

For $p \geq 1$, define

$$M[p] = \max_{i \in V \setminus F[p]} v_i[p] \tag{4.3}$$

and

$$m[p] = \min_{i \in V \setminus F[p]} v_i[p]. \tag{4.4}$$

We will prove that, given any $\epsilon > 0$, there exists τ such that

$$M[p] - m[p] \leq \epsilon \quad \forall p \geq \tau. \tag{4.5}$$

Consider p-th phase, for some $p \geq 0$. If $M[p] - m[p] = 0$, then the algorithm has already converged, and the proof is complete, with $\tau = p$.

Now consider the case when $M[p] - m[p] > 0$. Partition V into two subsets, A and B, such that, for each fault-free node $i \in A$, $v_i[p] \in \left[m[p], \frac{M[p]+m[p]}{2}\right)$, and for each fault-free node $j \in B$, $v_j[p] \in \left[\frac{M[p]+m[p]}{2}, M[p]\right]$. By definition of $m[p]$ and $M[p]$, there exist fault-free nodes i and j such that $v_i[p] = m[p]$ and $v_j[p] = M[p]$. Thus, sets A and B are both non-empty. By Lemma 4.7, one of the following two conditions must be true.

- Set A propagates to set B. Then, define $L = B$ and $R = A$. The states of all the fault-free nodes in $R = A$ are confined within an interval of length $< \frac{M[p]+m[p]}{2} - m[p] \leq \frac{M[p]-m[p]}{2}$.

- Set B propagates to set A. Then, define $L = A$ and $R = B$. In this case, states of all the fault-free nodes in $R = B$ are confined within an interval of length $\leq M[p] - \frac{M[p]+m[p]}{2} \leq \frac{M[p]-m[p]}{2}$.

In both cases above, we have found non-empty sets L and R such that (i) L, R is a partition of V, (ii) R propagates to L, and (iii) the states of all fault-free nodes in R are confined to an interval of length $\leq \frac{M[p]-m[p]}{2}$. Suppose that R propagates to L in $l(p)$ steps, where $l(p) \geq 1$. Then by Lemma 4.8,

$$M[p + l(p)] - m[p + l(p)] \leq \left(1 - \frac{\alpha^{l(p)}}{2}\right)(M[p] - m[p]). \tag{4.6}$$

Observe that $\alpha > 0$ (defined in Lemma 4.8), else Condition CCA-I is violated. Then, $n - f - 1 \geq l(p) \geq 1$ and $0 < \alpha \leq 1$; hence, $0 \leq \left(1 - \frac{\alpha^{l(p)}}{2}\right) < 1$.

Let us define the following sequence of phase indices:

- $\tau_0 = 0$,

- for $i > 0$, $\tau_i = \tau_{i-1} + l(\tau_{i-1})$, where $l(p)$ for any given p was defined above.

If for some i, $M[\tau_i] - m[\tau_i] = 0$, then since the algorithm satisfies the validity condition, we will have $M[t] - m[t] = 0$ for all $t \geq \tau_i$, and the proof of convergence is complete.

Now suppose that $M[\tau_i] - m[\tau_i] \neq 0$ for the values of i in the analysis below. By repeated application of the argument leading to (4.6), we can prove that, for $i \geq 0$,

$$M[\tau_i] - m[\tau_i] \leq \left(\prod_{j=1}^{i}\left(1 - \frac{\alpha^{\tau_j - \tau_{j-1}}}{2}\right)\right)(M[0] - m[0]). \tag{4.7}$$

For a given ϵ, by choosing a large enough i, we can obtain

$$\left(\prod_{j=1}^{i}\left(1 - \frac{\alpha^{\tau_j - \tau_{j-1}}}{2}\right)\right)(M[0] - m[0]) \leq \epsilon$$

and, therefore,

$$M[\tau_i] - m[\tau_i] \leq \epsilon. \tag{4.8}$$

For $p \geq \tau_i$, by validity of Algorithm LocWA, it follows that

$$M[p] - m[p] \leq M[\tau_i] - m[\tau_i] \leq \epsilon,$$

which proves that the algorithm will ϵ-converge by phase τ_i. Specifically, regarding the termination of LocWA we observe that Equation (4.7) together with the fact that $M[0] - m[0] \leq K$ implies that:

$$M[\tau_i] - m[\tau_i] \leq \left(\prod_{j=1}^{i}\left(1 - \frac{\alpha^{\tau_j - \tau_{j-1}}}{2}\right)\right)K$$

so, ϵ-convergence will be achieved in phase τ_i, where $\prod_{j=1}^{i} \left(1 - \frac{\alpha^{\tau_j - \tau_{j-1}}}{2}\right) K \leq \epsilon$. Since $\tau_j - \tau_{j-1} = l(\tau_j - 1) \leq n - f - 1$ for every j, we have that

$$\prod_{j=1}^{i} \left(1 - \frac{\alpha^{\tau_j - \tau_{j-1}}}{2}\right) K \leq \epsilon \Rightarrow \left(1 - \frac{\alpha^{n-f-1}}{2}\right)^i K \leq \epsilon \Rightarrow i \geq \log_{\left(1 - \frac{\alpha^{n-f-1}}{2}\right)} \frac{\epsilon}{K} \Rightarrow$$

$$\Rightarrow i \geq \frac{\log(\epsilon/K)}{\log\left(1 - \frac{\alpha^{n-f-1}}{2}\right)}.$$

By the definition of the sequence τ_i and the bound of all $l(p)$ we have that $\tau_i \leq i(n - f - 1)$. Thus, the algorithm will ϵ-converge by phase $\dfrac{\log(\epsilon/K)}{\log\left(1 - \frac{\alpha^{n-f-1}}{2}\right)}(n - f - 1)$ the latest.

This proves the correctness of LocWA for any $p_{end} > \dfrac{(n - f - 1)\log(\epsilon/K)}{\log\left(1 - \frac{\alpha_k^{n-f-1}}{2}\right)}$.

$\square$

4.3   GENERAL APPROXIMATE CONSENSUS

In this section, we consider general solutions for the crash-tolerant approximate consensus. Condition CCA-G, presented in Definition 2.10 of Section 2.4, is proven to be necessary and sufficient for solving the crash-tolerant approximate consensus in directed graphs as shown in the following. The result first appeared in [93], and the proof is similar to the analogous theorems appearing in Section 3.2.

4.3.1   NECESSITY OF CONDITION CCA-G

Theorem 4.10   *Condition CCA-G is necessary for approximate crash-tolerant consensus in an asynchronous system.*

4.3.2   SUFFICIENCY OF CONDITION CCA-G

We show the sufficiency of Condition CCA-G constructively by presenting Algorithm 4.5 WA (Wait-and-Average), and proving its correctness. The algorithm, presented below, assumes that each process has the knowledge of the network topology, and the algorithm proceeds in *asynchronous* phases. In each phase, processes flood messages containing the current value of their state variable v, their identifier, and a phase index. Each process i waits until it has received an "adequate" set of values from other processes, where "adequate" is made precise by Condition WAIT defined below. Then, process i updates its state variable v to be the *average* of set of values received in the current phase, and then proceeds to the next phase. When process i has finished p_{end} phases, it produces an output that equals the current value of state variable v; p_{end} is an integer $> \log_{n/(n-1)} \frac{K}{\epsilon}$.

In Algorithm WA, observe that $heard_i[p]$ is the set of processes from which process i has received values during phase p. As seen in the algorithm pseudo-code, process i performs the averaging operation to update its state variable v_i if Condition WAIT below holds for the first time. Algorithm WA is an extension of an approximate consensus algorithm for complete graphs [28] and is presented in [93]. The key difference lies in the identification of *Condition WAIT*.

Definition 4.11   Condition WAIT.   For $F_i \subseteq V$, where $|F_i| \leq f$, denote by $reach_i(F_i)$ the set of processes that have paths to process i in the subgraph induced by the processes in $V \setminus F_i$ (i.e., the paths do not contain processes in F_i). Condition *WAIT* is satisfied at process i if **there exists** a set $F_i \subseteq V$, where $|F_i| \leq f$, such that $reach_i(F_i) \subseteq heard_i[p]$. ($reach_i(F_i)$ may be different in each phase, since it depends on the message delays. For simplicity, we ignore the phase index p in the notation.)

Note that $R_i[p]$ is a multiset, and thus may contain multiple instances of the same value.

Correctness of Algorithm WA   We first prove a useful lemma. Let $heard_i^*[p]$ denote the set $heard_i[p]$ when Condition WAIT holds for the first time at process i in phase p. The correctness of Algorithm WA relies on the following lemma, which assumes graph $G = (V, E)$ satisfies Condition CCA-G. In a given execution, define $F[p]$ as the processes that have *not* computed value $v[p]$ in phase p, i.e., processes in $F[p]$ have crashed before computing $v[p]$.

Lemma 4.12   *For phase $p \geq 1$, consider two processes $i, j \in V \setminus F[p]$. Then, $heard_i^*[p] \cap heard_j^*[p] \neq \emptyset$.*

Proof. By construction, there exist two sets F_i and F_j such that Condition WAIT holds for sets $heard_i^*[p]$ and F_i at process i, and for sets $heard_j^*[p]$ and F_j at process j. In other words, (i) $F_i \subseteq V$ and $|F_i| \leq f$, (ii) $F_j \subseteq V$ and $|F_j| \leq f$, (iii) $reach_i(F_i) \subseteq heard_i^*[p]$, and (iv) $reach_j(F_j) \subseteq heard_j^*[p]$. If $reach_i(F_i) \cap reach_j(F_j) \neq \emptyset$, then the proof is complete, since $reach_i(F_i) \subseteq heard_i^*[p]$ and $reach_j(F_j) \subseteq heard_j^*[p]$. Thus, $heard_i^*[p] \cap heard_j^*[p] \neq \emptyset$.

Now, consider the case when $reach_i(F_i) \cap reach_j(F_j) = \emptyset$. We will derive a contradiction in this case. Recall that $reach_i(F_i)$ is defined as the set of processes that have paths to process i in the subgraph induced by the processes in $V \setminus F_i$. This implies that in graph G, the incoming neighbors of set $reach_i(F_i)$ are contained in set F_i. Similarly, in graph G, the incoming neighbors of set $reach_j(F_j)$ are contained in set F_j.

In graph G, we will find subsets of processes L, C, R that violate Condition CCA-G. Let $L = reach_i(F_i)$, $R = reach_j(F_j)$ and $C = V - L - R$. Observe that since $reach_i(F_i) \cap reach_j(F_j) = \emptyset$, L, C, R form a partition of V. Moreover, $i \in reach_i(F_i)$ and $j \in reach_j(F_j)$;

Algorithm 4.5 WA (Wait-and-Average)

(For process $i \in V$)

Initialization: $v_i[0] :=$ input at process i

Constant: $p_{end} > \log_{n/(n-1)} \frac{K}{\epsilon}$

1: **for** phase $p := 1$ **to** p_{end} **do**
2:     $R_i[p] := \{v_i[p-1]\}$
3:     $heard_i[p] := \{i\}$
4:     Send message $(v_i[p-1], i, p)$ to all the outgoing neighbors
5:     **repeat**
6:         **if** message (h, j, p) is received for the *first time*, **then**
7:             $R_i[p] := R_i[p] \cup \{h\}$ $\triangleright$ $R_i[p]$ is a multiset
8:             $heard_i[p] := heard_i[p] \cup \{j\}$
9:             Send message (h, j, p) to all the outgoing neighbors.
10:         **end if**
11:     **until** Condition WAIT is satisfied
12:     Update state as:

$$v_i[p] := \frac{\sum_{v \in R_i[p]} v}{|R_i[p]|}$$

13: **end for**
14: **output** $v_i[p]$

---

hence, $L = reach_i(F_i)$ and $R = reach_j(F_j)$ are both non-empty. Let $N(L)$ be the set of incoming neighbors of set L. By definition, $N(L)$ is contained in $R \cup C$. Since $L = reach_i(F_i)$, the only processes that may be in $N(L)$ are also in F_i as argued above, i.e., $N(L) \subseteq F_i$. By assumption, $|F_i| \leq f$. Therefore, $|N(L)| \leq f$, which implies that $R \cup C \overset{f+1}{\not\rightarrow} L$. Similarly, we can argue that $L \cup C \overset{f+1}{\not\rightarrow} R$. These two conditions together show that G violates Condition CCA-G, a contradiction. Thus, $reach_i(F_i) \cap reach_j(F_j) \neq \emptyset$, which implies that $heard_i^*[p] \cap heard_j^*[p] \neq \emptyset$. This completes the proof. $\qquad\square$

The next theorem states the correctness of Algorithm WA. Its proof is similar to the proof of Theorem 3.6.

Theorem 4.13 *Algorithm WA satisfies termination, ϵ-agreement, and validity properties.*

CHAPTER 5

Byzantine Fault Tolerance

In this chapter, we discuss Byzantine consensus algorithms in both synchronous and asynchronous systems. We first discuss implications of the related results and introduce a useful notion—reduced graphs. Then, we present the results on iterative algorithms (using Definitions 2.14 and 2.15) followed by general algorithms (using Definition 2.11).

5.1 IMPLICATIONS OF CONDITIONS BCS-I AND BCS-G

First, we present the lower bounds on the overall number of processes implied by Conditions BCS-I, BCS-G, and BCA-I. These are well-known results in complete and undirected graphs, e.g., [6, 58]. However, the implication shows that the conditions strictly generalize the known bounds in the case of directed incomplete networks. We summarize the bounds in the theorem presented below.

Theorem 5.1   *Conditions BCS-G and BCS-I imply that $n \geq 3f + 1$.*

Proof. We first present the proof for the case of BCS-G. Suppose that $2 \leq n \leq 3f$ and Condition BCS-G holds. Consider the following two cases.

- $2 \leq n \leq 2f$: Suppose that L, R, F is a partition of V such that $|L| = \lceil n/2 \rceil \leq f, |R| = \lfloor n/2 \rfloor \leq f$ and $F = \emptyset$. Note that L and R are non-empty, and $|L| + |R| = n$.

- $2f < n \leq 3f$: Suppose that L, R, F is a partition of V, such that $|L| = |R| = f$ and $|F| = n - 2f$. Note that $0 < |F| \leq f$.

Since Condition BCS-G holds, it means that either $L \cup C \overset{f+1}{\rightarrowtail} R$ or $R \cup C \overset{f+1}{\rightarrowtail} L$ holds in both the above cases. For $L \cup C \overset{f+1}{\rightarrowtail} R$ to be true, L must contain at least $f + 1$ nodes. Similarly, for $R \cup C \overset{f+1}{\rightarrowtail} L$ to be true, R must contain at least $f + 1$ nodes. Therefore, at least one of the sets L and R must contain more than f nodes. This contradicts our choice of L and R above (in both cases, size of L and R is smaller than f). Therefore, n must be larger than $3f$.

The case of BCS-I holds analogously to the first case. $\square$

The following theorem can be proved similarly.

Theorem 5.2   *Condition BCA-I implies $n \geq 5f + 1$.*

The following theorem presents the relations between the conditions BCS-I, BCS-G and BCA-I and the conditions that were studied in the previous chapters.

Theorem 5.3

1. *BCA-I strictly implies BCS-I.*

2. *BCS-I strictly implies BCS-G.*

3. *BCS-I strictly implies CCA-I.*

4. *BCS-G strictly implies CCA-G.*

5. *None of BCS-G, CCA-I implies the other.*

Proof.

1. By definition, Condition BCS-I can be viewed as a special case of Condition BCA-I since for any sets A, B it holds that $A \xrightarrow{2f+1} B$ implies $A \xrightarrow{f+1} B$.

   To see that the conditions are not equivalent, consider the clique K_{3f+1} of size $3f + 1$. It is trivial to see that BCS-I holds in K_{3f+1} while BCA-I does not.

2. By definition, it holds that for any sets of nodes A, B, $A \xrightarrow{f+1} B$ implies $A \xrightarrow{f+1} B$. Since this is the only difference in the definition of Conditions BCS-I, BCS-G, it follows that BCS-I implies BCS-G.

   To see that the conditions are not equivalent consider Figure 2.4 for $f = 2$. In this network, BCS-G is satisfied since the removal of any 2-node set F will leave at least 3 directed edges from K_1 to K_2 or the vice versa. On the other hand, Condition BCS-I is not satisfied in this network for any 2-node set F and $L = K_1 \setminus F, R = K_2 \setminus F, C = \emptyset$.

3. By definition, Condition CCA-I can be viewed as a special case of Condition BCS-I for $F = \emptyset$.

   A clique consisting of $2f + 1$ nodes satisfies Condition CCA-I but not Condition BCS-I; thus, Condition CCA-I does not imply BCS-I.

4. Similar to the proof of point 3.

5. Similarly with the proof of point 2, BCS-G holds in the network of Figure 2.4 for $f = 2$ while CCA-I does not. This proves that CCA-I $\not\Rightarrow$ BCS-G.

   Moreover, a clique of $2f + 1$ nodes satisfies CCA-I but not BCS-G. This shows that BCS-G $\not\Rightarrow$ CCA-I.

$\square$

5.2   REDUCED GRAPH

Similar to what we saw in Chapter 3, the conditions imply that there exists some graph that allows the information propagation after the removal of faulty processes. Vaidya et al. [98] first proposed the notion of "reduced graph" to capture such information propagation. Reduced graph are later used in series of works, e.g., [86, 93].

We first discuss some standard concept from graph theory to facilitate the discussion.

Definition 5.4   Graph Decomposition.   Let H be a directed graph. Partition graph H into non-empty strongly connected components, $H_1, H_2, \cdots, H_h$, where h is a non-zero integer dependent on graph H, such that

- every pair of nodes within the same strongly connected component has directed paths in H to each other; and

- for each pair of nodes, say i and j, that belong to two *different* strongly connected components, either i does not have a directed path to j in H, or j does not have a directed path to i in H.

Construct a graph H^d wherein each strongly connected component H_k above is represented by vertex c_k, and there is an edge from vertex c_k to vertex c_l if and only if the nodes in H_k have directed paths in H to the nodes in H_l. It is known that the decomposition graph H^d is a

directed *acyclic* graph [24].

Definition 5.5   Source Component.   Let H be a directed graph, and let H^d be its decomposition as per Definition 5.4. Strongly connected component H_k of H is said to be a *source component* if the corresponding vertex c_k in H^d is <u>not</u> reachable from any other vertex in H^d.

Now we are ready to formally define the notion of reduced graph.

Definition 5.6   Reduced Graph.   For a given graph $G = (V, E)$ and $F \subset V$, a graph $G_F(V_F, E_F)$ is said to be a *reduced graph*, if: (i) $V_F = V \setminus F$, and (ii) E_F is obtained by first removing from E all the links incident on the processes in F, and *then* removing up to f other incoming links at each process in V_F.

Note that for a given $G = (V, E)$, multiple reduced graphs G_F may exist.

The following theorem shows the implication of Condition BCS-I. Using similar technique, one can prove that the condition below is in fact equivalent to Condition BCS-I. The full proof is presented in [87].

Theorem 5.7   *Suppose that Condition BCS-I holds for graph $G = (V, E)$. Then, for any $F \subset V$ such that $|F| < |V|$ and $|F| \le f$, every reduced graph G_F obtained as per Definition 5.6 must contain exactly one source component.*

Proof. Since $|F| < |V|$, G_F contains at least one process; therefore, at least one source component must exist in G_F. We now prove that G_F cannot contain more than one source component. The proof is by contradiction. Suppose that there exists a set $F \subset V$ with $|F| < |V|$ and $|F| \leq f$, and a reduced graph $G_F(V_F, E_F)$ corresponding to F, such that the decomposition of G_F includes at least two source components.

Let the sets of processes in two such source components of G_F be denoted L and R, respectively. Let $C = V \setminus (F \cup L \cup R)$. Observe that F, L, C, R form a partition of the processes in V. Since L is a source component in G_F it follows that there are no directed links in E_F from any process in $C \cup R$ to the processes in L. Similarly, since R is a source component in G_F it follows that there are no directed links in E_F from any process in $L \cup C$ to the processes in R. These observations, together with the manner in which E_F is defined, imply that (i) there are at most f links in E from the processes in $C \cup R$ to each process in L, and (ii) there are at most f links in E from the processes in $L \cup C$ to each process in R. Therefore, in graph $G = (V, E)$, $C \cup R \overset{f+1}{\not\twoheadrightarrow} L$ and $C \cup L \overset{f+1}{\not\twoheadrightarrow} R$, violating Condition BCS-I. Thus, we have proved that G_F must contain exactly one source component. $\qquad\square$

Intuitively, the removal of processes in F is to isolate the set of faulty processes. Observe that we remove edges from each process while constructing the reduced graph. These additional removal of edges is because that each process is "memory-less," and to satisfy validity, it needs to discard additional values. In certain scenarios, each process will never learn useful information from the removed edges. This intuition will become clear in the discussion of necessity proof and the algorithm.

There is another notion of reduced graphs, namely *general reduced graph*. In this family of reduced graphs, one needs to remove processes and edges in a different way as presented below.

Definition 5.8   General Reduced Graph.   For a given graph $G = (V, E)$, and sets $F \subset V$, $F_1 \subset V \setminus F$, such that $|F| \leq f$ and $|F_1| \leq f$, reduced graph $G_{F,F_1} = (V_{F,F_1}, E_{F,F_1})$ is defined as follows: (i) $V_{F,F_1} = V \setminus F$ and (ii) E_{F,F_1} is obtained by removing from E all the links incident on the processes in F, and all the outgoing links from processes in F_1. That is, $E_{F,F_1} = E \setminus \{(i, j) \mid i \in F \text{ or } j \in F\} \setminus \{(i, j) \mid i \in F_1\}$.

The main difference between reduced graph (in Definition 5.6) and general reduced graph is that we need to remove the outgoing links from additional processes (i.e., processes in F_1). The intuition is that under general algorithms, faulty processes (say in F) can behave as in an execution where processes in some other set (say in F_1) are faulty. Consequently, for other processes (say in $V \setminus (F \cup F_1)$), they need to be able to "exchange information" and derive decision without using either set. Moreover, if the processes in F_1 are indeed fault-free, then they need a way to learn the final decision from other nodes in $V \setminus F$. Therefore, we do *not* remove their incoming links.

In the same spirit of Theorem 5.7, it is not hard to derive the following theorem.

Theorem 5.9   *Suppose that Condition BCS-G holds for graph $G = (V, E)$. Then, for any $|F| \leq f$ and $|F_1| \leq f$, every general reduced graph G_{F,F_1} obtained as per Definition 5.8 must contain exactly one source component.*

The proof is similar to the one of Theorem 5.7; hence, we leave that as an exercise for interested readers. Moreover, it is also straightforward to prove that this condition is equivalent to Condition BCS-G whose proof is presented in [87].

5.3   ITERATIVE APPROXIMATE CONSENSUS

Here, we first show the result in synchronous systems, which was first presented in [98].

5.3.1   NECESSITY OF CONDITION BCS-I

For a correct IAC algorithm to exist, the underlying graph $G = (V, E)$ must satisfy Condition BCS-I as stated in Theorem 2.14.

Proof. The proof is by contradiction. Let us assume that a correct iterative consensus algorithm exists, and $C \cup R \stackrel{f+1}{\not\twoheadrightarrow} L$ and $L \cup C \stackrel{f+1}{\not\twoheadrightarrow} R$. Thus, for any $i \in L, |N_i^- \cap (C \cup R)| < f + 1$, and for any $j \in R, |N_j^- \cap (L \cup C)| < f + 1$. Figure 5.1 illustrates the sets used in this proof.

Also assume that the processes in F (if F is non-empty) are all faulty, and the other processes in sets L, C, R are fault-free. Note that the fault-free processes are not aware of the identity of the faulty processes.

Consider the case when (i) each process in L has initial input m, (ii) each process in R has initial input M, such that $M > m$, and (iii) each process in C, if C is non-empty, has an input in the interval $[m, M]$.

In the *Transmit Step* of iteration 1, suppose that the faulty processes in F (if non-empty) send $m^- < m$ on outgoing links to processes in L, send $M^+ > M$ on outgoing links to processes in R, and send some arbitrary value in interval $[m, M]$ on outgoing links to the processes in C (if C is non-empty). This behavior is possible since processes in F are faulty. Note that $m^- < m < M < M^+$. Each fault-free process $k \in V \setminus F$, sends to processes in N_k^+ value $v_k[0]$ in iteration 1.

Consider any process $i \in L$. Denote $N_i' = N_i^- \cap (C \cup R)$. Since $|F| \leq f, |N_i^- \cap F| \leq f$.

Since $C \cup R \stackrel{f+1}{\not\twoheadrightarrow} L, |N_i'| \leq f$. Node i will then receive m^- from the processes in $N_i^- \cap F$, and values in $[m, M]$ from the processes in N_i', and m from the processes in $\{i\} \cup (N_i^- \cap L)$.

Consider the following two cases.

- Both $N_i^- \cap F$ and N_i' are non-empty: Now $|N_i^- \cap F| \leq f$ and $|N_i'| \leq f$. From process i's perspective, consider two possible scenarios: (a) processes in $N_i^- \cap F$ are faulty, and the

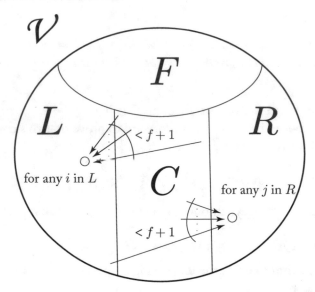

Figure 5.1: Illustration for the necessity proof of Theorem 2.14. The case of $C \cup R \overset{f+1}{\not\twoheadrightarrow} L$ and $L \cup C \overset{f+1}{\not\twoheadrightarrow} R$.

other processes are fault-free, and (b) processes in N_i' are faulty, and the other processes are fault-free.

In scenario (a), from process i's perspective, the faulty-free processes have sent values in interval $[m, M]$, whereas the faulty processes have sent value m^-. According to the validity condition, $v_i[1] \geq m$. On the other hand, in scenario (b), the fault-free processes have sent values m^- and m, where $m^- < m$; so $v_i[1] \leq m$, according to the validity condition. Since process i does not know whether the correct scenario is (a) or (b), it must update its state to satisfy the validity condition in both cases. Thus, it follows that $v_i[1] = m$.

- At most one of $N_i^- \cap F$ and N_i' is non-empty: Thus, $|(N_i^- \cap F) \cup N_i'| \leq f$. From process i's perspective, it is possible that the processes in $(N_i^- \cap F) \cup N_i'$ are all faulty, and the rest of the processes are fault-free. In this situation, the values sent to process i by the fault-free processes (which are all in $\{i\} \cup (N_i^- \cap L)$) are all m, and therefore, $v_i[1]$ must be set to m as per the validity condition.

Thus, $v_i[1] = m$ for each process $i \in L$. Similarly, we can show that $v_j[1] = M$ for each process $j \in R$.

Now consider the processes in set C, if C is non-empty. All the values received by the processes in C are in $[m, M]$, therefore, their new state must also remain in $[m, M]$, as per the validity condition.

The above discussion implies that, at the end of iteration 1, the following conditions hold true: (i) state of each process in L is m, (ii) state of each process in R is M, and (iii) state of each process in C is in the interval $[m, M]$. These conditions are identical to the initial conditions listed previously. Then, by a repeated application of the above argument (proof by induction), it follows that for any $t \geq 0$, $v_i[t] = m$ for all $\forall i \in L$, $v_j[t] = M$ for all $j \in R$ and $v_k[t] \in [m, M]$ for all $k \in C$.

Since L and R both contain fault-free processes, the convergence requirement is not satisfied. This is a contradiction to the assumption that a correct iterative algorithm exists.   □

5.3.2   SUFFICIENCY OF CONDITION BCS-I

We will prove that there exists an IAC algorithm—particularly Algorithm IBS (Iterative Byzantine Synchronous) 5.6, presented below—that satisfies the *validity* and *convergence* conditions provided that the graph $G = (V, E)$ satisfies Condition BCS-I. Algorithm 5.6 has the three-step structure described in Chapter 2, and it is similar to algorithms that were analyzed in prior work as well [28, 58]. The termination of the algorithm can be guaranteed with its slight modification in a way similar to [28, 58]. Similar to the proof of Theorem 4.9, with $M[t], m[t]$ we will denote the maximum and the minimum state values of players in $V \setminus \mathcal{F}$ at the end of the t-th iteration, iteratively.

Theorem 5.10   *Suppose that $\mathcal{F}$ is the set of Byzantine faulty processes, and that $G = (V, E)$ satisfies the* sufficient *condition stated above. Then Algorithm 5.6 satisfies the* validity *condition.*

Proof.   Consider the t-th iteration, and any fault-free process $i \in V \setminus \mathcal{F}$. Consider the following two cases.

- $f = 0$: In this case, all processes must be fault-free, and $\mathcal{F} = \emptyset$. In (5.1) in Algorithm 5.6, note that $v_i[t]$ is computed using states from the previous iteration at process i and other processes. By definition of $m[t-1]$ and $M[t-1]$, $v_j[t-1] \in [m[t-1], M[t-1]]$ for all fault-free processes $j \in V \setminus \mathcal{F}$. Thus, in this case, all the values used in computing $v_i[t]$ are in the interval $[m[t-1], M[t-1]]$. Since $v_i[t]$ is computed as a weighted average of these values, $v_i[t]$ is also within $[m[t-1], M[t-1]]$.

- $f > 0$: It is easy to see that Condition BCS-I implies that $|N_i^-| \geq 2f + 1$; therefore, $|r_i[t]| \geq 2f + 1$. When computing set $N_i^*[t]$, the largest f and smallest f values from $r_i[t]$ are eliminated. Since at most f processes are faulty, it follows that, either (i) the values received from the faulty processes are all eliminated, or (ii) the values from the faulty processes that still remain are between values received from two fault-free processes. Thus, the remaining values in $r_i[t]$ are all in the interval $[m[t-1], M[t-1]]$. Also, $v_i[t-1]$ is in $[m[t-1], M[t-1]]$, as per the definition of $m[t-1]$ and $M[t-1]$. Thus, $v_i[t]$ is computed as a weighted average of values in $[m[t-1], M[t-1]]$, and, therefore, it will also be in $[m[t-1], M[t-1]]$.

Algorithm 5.6 IBS (Iterative-Byzantine-Synchronous)

(For process $i \in V$)

Initialization: $v_i[0] :=$ input of node i

1: *Transmit step:* Transmit current state $v_i[t-1]$ on all outgoing edges.

2: *Receive step:* Receive values on all incoming edges. These values form vector $r_i[t]$ of size $|N_i^-|$. When a fault-free process expects to receive a message from a neighbor but does not receive the message, the message value is assumed to be equal to some *default value*.

3: *Update step:* Sort the values in $r_i[t]$ in an increasing order, and eliminate the smallest f values, and the largest f values (breaking ties arbitrarily). Let $N_i^*[t]$ denote the set of processes from whom the remaining $|N_i^-| - 2f$ values were received, and let w_j denote the value received from process $j \in N_i^*$. For convenience, define $w_i = v_i[t-1]$ to be the value process i "receives" from itself. Observe that if $j \in \{i\} \cup N_i^*[t]$ is fault-free, then $w_j = v_j[t-1]$. Define

$$v_i[t] = Z_i(r_i[t]) = \sum_{j \in \{i\} \cup N_i^*[t]} a_i \, w_j, \tag{5.1}$$

where

$$a_i = \frac{1}{|N_i^-| + 1 - 2f}$$

Note that $|N_i^*[t]| = |N_i^-| - 2f$, and $i \notin N_i^*[t]$ because $(i,i) \notin E$. The "weight" of each term on the right-hand side of (5.1) is a_i, and these weights add to 1. Also, $0 < a_i \le 1$. For future reference, let us define α as:

$$\alpha = \min_{i \in V} a_i \tag{5.2}$$

Since $\forall i \in V \setminus \mathcal{F}$, $v_i[t] \in [m[t-1], M[t-1]]$, the validity condition is satisfied. $\qquad \square$

For the convergence property, the proof is similar to the one in Chapter 4. Hence, we only present the key lemmas without showing the proof details. The interested reader can refer to [98] for more details.

Using a similar notion of propagating sequence from Definition 4.6, we can derive the following lemma.

Lemma 5.11 *Assume that $G = (V, E)$ satisfies Condition BCS-I. For any partition A, B, F of V, where A, B are both non-empty, and $|F| \le f$, either A propagates to B, or B propagates to A.*

Lemma 5.11 can be used to prove the following lemma. Recall that α is defined in (5.2). Moreover, $M[p]$ and $m[p]$ denote the maximum and minimum states at the fault-free process at the end of the p-th iteration.

Lemma 5.12 *Using Algorithm 5.6, we have*

$$M[s + l] - m[s + l] \leq \left(1 - \frac{\alpha^l}{2}\right)(M[s] - m[s]) \tag{5.3}$$

if all the following conditions hold:

- *$G = (V, E)$ satisfies Condition BCS-I;*

- *$\mathcal{F}$ is the set of Byzantine faulty processes; and*

- *at the end of the s-th iteration of Algorithm 5.6, the fault-free processes in $V - \mathcal{F}$ can be partitioned into non-empty sets R and L such that (i) R propagates to L in l steps, and (ii) the states of processes in R are confined to an interval of length $\leq \frac{M[s]-m[s]}{2}$.*

Similar to what we saw in Chapter 4, Lemma 5.12 implies that Algorithm 5.6 satisfies the convergence property. Observe that, as the algorithm is stated, no termination occurs; thus, the proof presented argues that there exists some round in which the state values of all fault-free processes will be in distance ϵ from each other. However, the termination property can be shown to hold in the same way it holds for analogous algorithms presented in [28, 44, 58].

5.3.3 CONDITION BCA-I

Now, we focus on the asynchronous iterative approximate consensus algorithms. Recall that in Section 1.4.2, we discuss the difference between asynchronous IAC and synchronous IAC algorithms. Intuitively, in asynchronous IAC algorithms, each process proceeds in (asynchronous) phases. Each message is tagged with phase index, and processes need to receive enough number of messages in the same phase to proceed to the update phase.

Necessity Intuitively, the necessity proof of Condition BCA-I (Theorem 2.15) is a combination of necessity proof of Condition BCS-I and Condition BCA-I. Assume that by way of contradiction, a correct Asynchronous IAC consensus algorithm exists in G, in which $C \cup R \overset{2f+1}{\not\rightarrow} L$ and $C \cup L \overset{2f+1}{\not\rightarrow} R$. Thus, for any $i \in L$, $|N_i^- \cap (C \cup R)| < 2f + 1$, and for any $j \in R$, $|N_j^- \cap (L \cup C)| < 2f + 1$ in G. Consider the case when (i) each node in L has input m, (ii) each node in R has input M, such that $M > m$, and (iii) each node in C, if C is non-empty, has an input in the range $[m, M]$. Fix a process $i \in L$. Then consider the case that the messages from f of its neighbors in $C \cup R$ are so slow that process i has to ignore them (otherwise, termination property will be violated). Similarly, each process $j \in R$ has to ignore messages from f of its neighbors in $C \cup L$. And the rest of the proof is similar to proof of Condition BCS-I.

Sufficiency Tseng et al. [87] presented an Asynchronous IAC algorithm—Algorithm IBA (Iterative-Byzantine-Asynchonous) 5.7 below—that satisfies the *validity* and *convergence* conditions provided that the graph $G = (V, E)$ satisfies Condition BCA-I. Algorithm 5.7 has the three-step structure, and it is similar to algorithms that were analyzed in prior work as well [7, 28].

Algorithm 5.7 IBA (Iterative-Byzantine-Asynchonous)

(For process $i \in V$)
Initialization: $v_i[0] :=$ input of node i

1: *Transmit step:* Transmit current state $v_i[t-1]$ on all outgoing edges.

2: *Receive step:* Wait until receiving values on all but f incoming edges. These values form vector $r_i[t]$ of size $|N_i^-| - f$.

3: *Update step:* Sort the values in $r_i[t]$ in an increasing order, and eliminate the smallest f values, and the largest f values (breaking ties arbitrarily). Let $N_i^*[t]$ denote the identifiers of processes from whom the remaining $N_i^- - 3f$ values were received, and let w_j denote the value received from process $j \in N_i^*$. For convenience, define $w_i = v_i[t-1]$ to be the value process i "receives" from itself. Observe that if $j \in \{i\} \cup N_i^*[t]$ is fault-free, then $w_j = v_j[t-1]$.
Define

$$v_i[t] = Z_i(r_i[t], v_i[t-1]) = \sum_{j \in \{i\} \cup N_i^*[t]} a_i\, w_j, \qquad (5.4)$$

where

$$a_i = \frac{1}{|N_i^-| + 1 - 3f}$$

Note that $|N_i^*[t]| = |N_i^-| - 3f$, and $i \notin N_i^*[t]$ because $(i, i) \notin \mathcal{E}$. The "weight" of each term on the right-hand side of (5.4) is a_i, and these weights add to 1. Also, $0 < a_i \le 1$. For future reference, let us define α as:

$$\alpha = \min_{i \in \mathcal{V}} a_i \qquad (5.5)$$

5.4 GENERAL ALGORITHMS

In this section, we only present the results in synchronous systems, as the *tight* condition in asynchronous systems remains open.

5.4.1 NECESSITY OF CONDITION BCS-G

In previous sections, we consider a specific family of *iterative* algorithms—IAC algorithms. In the discussion below, we explore general algorithms. The key benefits include full topology knowledge and capability to route messages and store general information. Condition BCS-G is proven to be necessary using the indistinguishability argument [4, 30]. Here, we present the proof sketch. Please refer to [90] for the full proof that used proof by contradiction and the covering graph technique [30].

Proof Sketch: Suppose that there exists a partition L, C, R, F where L, R are non-empty and $|F| \leq f$ such that $L \cup C \overset{f+1}{\nrightarrow} R$ and $R \cup C \overset{f+1}{\nrightarrow} L$. Assume that the processes in F are all faulty, and the processes in sets L, C, R are fault-free. Note that fault-free processes are *not* aware of the identity of the faulty processes. Consider the case when all the processes in L have input m, and all the processes in $R \cup C$ have input M, where $m \neq M$. Suppose that the processes in F (if non-empty) behave to processes in L as if processes in $R \cup C \cup F$ have input m, while behaving to processes in R as if processes in $L \cup C \cup F$ have input M. This behavior by processes in F is possible, since the processes in F are all assumed to be faulty. Consider processes in L.

Let N_L denote the set of incoming neighbors of L in $R \cup C$. Since $R \cup C \overset{f+1}{\nrightarrow} LL, |N_L| \leq f$. Therefore, processes in L cannot distinguish between the following two scenarios:

- all the processes in N_L (if non-empty) are faulty, rest of the processes are fault-free, and all the fault-free processes have input m; and

- all the processes in F (if non-empty) are faulty, rest of the processes are fault-free, and fault-free processes have input either m or M.

In the first scenario, for validity, the output at processes in L must be m. Therefore, in the second scenario as well, the output at the processes in L must be m. We can similarly show that the output at the processes in R must be M. Thus, if Condition BCS-G is not satisfied, processes in L and R can be forced to decide on distinct values, violating the agreement property. □

5.4.2 SUFFICIENCY OF CONDITION BCS-G

We focus on a Byzantine consensus algorithm for *binary* inputs, which must satisfy Agreement, Validity, and Termination property. Using this algorithm as a sub-routine, it is easy to devise a multi-valued Byzantine consensus algorithm that satisfies weak validity [48]: If all fault-free processes have the same input, then the output of every fault-free processes equals its input. We only present the intuition below, and please refer to [90] for the full proof.

When $f = 0$, Condition BCS-G implies that there must exist at least one process, say process i, that has directed paths to all the remaining processes in the system. Process i can route its input to all the other processes, and all the processes can adopt process i's input as the output. Recall that no process is faulty and in general algorithms, each process has the full topology knowledge. The aforementioned algorithm works correct based on these two observations. Detailed algorithm and proof on the case of $f = 0$ can be found in [90]. In the rest of our discussion below, we will assume that $f > 0$ and describe a Byzantine consensus algorithm, namely Algorithm BC.

Terminology

To facilitate the discussion, we introduce some useful notations regarding paths of the graph. We will only consider directed paths in our discussion.

- We will use the following notions regarding paths:

  - For a directed path from process i to process j, process i is said to be the "source node" for the path.

  - An "(i, j)-path" is a directed path from process i to process j.

  - An "(i, j)-path excluding X" is a directed path from process i to process j that does not contain any process from set X.

  - Two paths from process i to process j are said to be "disjoint" if the two paths only have processes i and j in common, with all remaining processes being distinct.

  - The phrase "d disjoint (i, j)-paths" refers to d pairwise disjoint paths from process i to process j.

  - The phrase "d disjoint (i, j)-paths excluding X" refers to d pairwise disjoint (i, j)-paths that do not contain any process from set X.

- Every process i trivially has a path to itself. That is, for all $i \in V$, an (i, i)-path excluding $V - \{i\}$ exists.

- Paths from a set S to process $j \notin S$ are as follows.

  - A path is said to be an "(S, j)-path" if it is an (i, j)-path for some $i \in S$.

  - An "(S, j)-path excluding X" is a (S, j)-path that does not contain any process from set X.

  - Two (S, j)-paths are said to be "disjoint" if the two paths only have process j in common, with all remaining processes being distinct (including the source nodes on the paths).

  - The phrase "d disjoint (S, j)-paths" refers to d pairwise disjoint (S, j)-paths.

  - The phrase "d disjoint (S, j)-paths excluding X" refers to d pairwise disjoint (S, j)-paths that do not contain any process from set X.

Using the aforementioned notion on directed paths, we now define an important notion over the given graph $G = (V, E)$.

Definition 5.13   Given disjoint subsets A, B, F of V such that $|F| \leq f$, set A is said to propagate in $V \setminus F$ to set B if either (i) $B = \emptyset$, or (ii) for each process $b \in B$, there exist at least $f + 1$ disjoint (A, b)-paths excluding F. We will denote the fact that set A propagates in

$V \setminus F$ to set B by the notation

$$A \overset{V \setminus F}{\leadsto} B.$$

When it is not true that $A \overset{V \setminus F}{\leadsto} B$, we will denote that fact by

$$A \overset{V \setminus F}{\not\leadsto} B.$$

Definition 5.14   Condition BCS-Prop.   For any partition of A, B, F of V such that A, B are non-empty and $|F| \leq f$, either $A \overset{V \setminus F}{\leadsto} B$ or $B \overset{V \setminus F}{\leadsto} A$.

By standard graph theory and Menger's Theorem [100], one can prove the following corollaries. Their full proofs are presented in [90].

Corollary 5.15   *Condition BCS-G is equivalent to Condition BCS-Prop.*

Corollary 5.16   *Assume that Condition BCS-G holds for $G = (V, E)$. For any partition A, B, F of V, where A is non-empty, and $|F| \leq f$, if $B \overset{f+1}{\not\leadsto} A$, then $A \overset{V \setminus F}{\leadsto} B$.*

Algorithm BC

We now present the description of Algorithm 5.8 BC (Byzantine-Consensus). In the discussion below, we assume that G satisfies Condition BCS-G. Due to Corollary 5.15, G also satisfies Condition BCS-Prop.

Variable   In Algorithm BC, each process i maintains two state variables that are explicitly used in the algorithm: v_i and t_i. Each process maintains other state as well (such as the routes to other processes and topology information); however, we do not introduce additional notation for that for simplicity.

- *Variable v_i:*

  Initially, v_i at any process i is equal to the binary input provided to process i. During the execution of the algorithm, v_i may be updated several times. At the end of the algorithm, each process i will output the value of v_i (or decides on v_i). Since we assume binary input, the output at each process is either 0 or 1. In fact, at any point of time, v_i is either 0 or 1.

Algorithm 5.8 BC (Byzantine-Consensus)

1: ▷ *OUTER LOOP*
2: **for all** $F \subset V$, where $0 \leq |F| \leq f$, **do**

3:      ▷ *INNER LOOP*
4:      **for all** partitions A, B of $V \setminus F$ such that A, B are non-empty, and $A \overset{V\setminus F}{\leadsto} B$, **do**

5:          ▷ *STEP 1 of INNER LOOP*
6:          **if** $A \overset{V\setminus F}{\leadsto} B$ and $B \overset{V\setminus F}{\not\leadsto} A$ **then**   ▷ **Case 1**
7:              Choose a non-empty set $S \subseteq A$ such that $S \overset{V\setminus F}{\leadsto} V \setminus (F \cup S)$, and S is strongly connected in G_F (G_F is defined in Definition 5.6)
8:                  (a) At each process $i \in S$:
9:                      $t_i := v_i$
10:                 (b) Equality(S)
11:                 (c) Propagate($S, V \setminus (F \cup S)$)
12:                 (d) At each process $j \in V \setminus (F \cup S)$:
13:                     if $t_j \neq \bot$, then $v_j := t_j$
14:         **else if** $A \overset{V\setminus F}{\leadsto} B$ and $B \overset{V\setminus F}{\leadsto} A$, **then**   ▷ **Case 2**
15:             Choose a non-empty set $S \subseteq A \cup B$ such that $S \overset{V\setminus F}{\leadsto} V \setminus (F \cup S)$, S is strongly connected in G_{-F}, and $A \overset{V\setminus F}{\leadsto} (S \setminus A)$.
16:                 (e) At each process $i \in A$:
17:                     $t_i := v_i$
18:                 (f) Propagate($A, S \setminus A$)
19:                 (g) Equality(S)
20:                 (h) Propagate($S, V \setminus (F \cup S)$)
21:                 (i) At each process $j \in V \setminus F \setminus (A \cap S)$:
22:                     if $t_j \neq \bot$, then $v_j := t_j$
23:         **end if**

24:         ▷ *STEP 2 of INNER LOOP*
25:         Each process $k \in F$ receives v_j from each $j \in N_k$, where N_k is a set consisting of $f + 1$ of k's incoming neighbors in $V \setminus F$. If all the received values are identical, then v_k is set equal to this identical value; else v_k is unchanged.
26:     **end for**
27: **end for**

At any time during the execution of the algorithm, the value v_i at process i is said to be *valid*, if it equals some fault-free process's input. By definition, initial value v_i at a fault-free process i is valid, because it equals its own input. Later on, we show that that v_i at a fault-free process i always remains valid throughout the execution of Algorithm BC.

- *Variable t_i:*

Variable t_i at any process i may take a value in $\{0, 1, \perp\}$, where $\perp$ is distinguished from 0 and 1. Algorithm BC makes use of procedures `Propagate` and `Equality` that are described soon below. These procedures take t_i as input, and possibly also modify t_i. Under some circumstances, as discussed later, state variable v_i at process i is set equal to t_i, in order to update v_i.

Algorithm Flow Algorithm 5.8 BC consists of two loops, an OUTER loop and an INNER loop. The OUTER loop chooses a subset of processes F, $|F| \leq f$, so that they will *not* participate in this iteration of the OUTER loop. For each iteration of the OUTER loop, many iterations of the INNER loop are performed. The processes in F do not participate in any of these INNER loop iterations. In other words, for a chosen F, each iteration of the INNER loop is performed for a different partition of $V \setminus F$.

Since there are at most f faults and Algorithm BC enumerates all possible F, one iteration of the OUTER loop has F exactly equal to the set of faulty processes. Denote the actual set of faulty processes as F^*. Algorithm BC has two properties, as proved later.

- State v_i of each fault-free process i at the end of any particular INNER loop iteration equals the state of some fault-free process at the start of that INNER loop iteration. Thus, Algorithm BC ensures that the state v_i of each fault-free process i remains valid at all times.

- By the end of the OUTER loop iteration for $F = F^*$, all the fault-free processes reach agreement.

The above two properties ensure that, when Algorithm BC terminates, the validity and agreement properties are both satisfied.

Each iteration of the INNER loop, for a given set F, considers a partition A, B of the processes in $V \setminus F$ such that $A \overset{V \setminus F}{\leadsto} B$. In other words, set A propagates in $V \setminus F$ to set B as per Definition 5.13. We can make such an assumption because of Corollary 5.15. Having chosen a partition A, B, intuitively speaking, the goal of the INNER loop iteration is for the processes in set A to "attempt to influence" the state of the processes in the other partition. A suitable set $S \subseteq A \cup B$ is identified and agreed *a priori* using the known topology information. There are two possible cases.

- In Case 1 in Algorithm BC, $S \subseteq A$, and processes in S use procedure `Equality` (step (b) in the pseudo-code) to decide the value to propagate to processes in $V \setminus (F \cup S)$ (step (c)).

- In Case 2, $S \subseteq A \cup B$, and processes in S first learn the states at processes in A using procedure Propagate (step (f)), and then use procedure Equality (step (g)) to decide the value to propagate to processes in $V \setminus (F \cup S)$ (step (h)).

These steps ensure that if $F = F^*$, and processes in A have the same v value, then S will propagate that value, and all processes in $V \setminus (F^* \cup S)$ (Case 1: step (d)) or in $V \setminus F^* \setminus (A \cap S)$ (Case 2: step (i)) will set v value equal to the value propagated by S, and thus, the agreement is achieved. As proved later, in at least one INNER loop iteration with $F = F^*$, processes in A will have the same v value.

Pseudo-code For clarity, the algorithm is presented in a centralized fashion in Algorithm 5.8. This simplifies some details like routing or accepting messages. However, Algorithm BC can be implemented in a distributive manner. Since we assume that each process knows the topology, processes can follow the predetermined schedule to perform each function distributively in Algorithm BC.

Procedures The two procedures, Propagate and ™Equality, used in Algorithm BC, are presented in Algorithms 5.9, 5.10, respectively.

Algorithm 5.9 Propagate (P, D)

1: Since $P \overset{V \setminus F}{\leadsto} D$, for each $i \in D$, there exist at least $f + 1$ disjoint (P, i)-paths that exclude F. The source process of each of these paths is in P. On each of $f + 1$ such disjoint paths, the source process for that path, say s, sends t_s to process i. Intermediate processes on these paths forward received messages as necessary.
   When a process does not receive an expected message, the message content is assumed to be $\perp$.

2: When any process $i \in D$ receives $f + 1$ values along the $f + 1$ disjoint paths above:

   - if the $f + 1$ values are all equal to 0, then $t_i := 0$;

   - else if the $f + 1$ values are all equal to 1, then $t_i := 1$;

   - else $t_i := \perp$.

   ▷ For any process $j \notin D$, t_j is not modified during Propagate(P, D). Also, for any process $k \in V$, v_k is not modified during Propagate(P, D).

Propagate(P, D) assumes that $P \subseteq V \setminus F$, $D \subseteq V \setminus F$, $P \cap D = \emptyset$ and $P \overset{V \setminus F}{\leadsto} D$. Recall that set F is the set chosen in each OUTER loop as specified by Algorithm BC.

   Equality(D) assumes that $D \subseteq V \setminus F$, $D \neq \emptyset$, and for each pair of processes $i, j \in D$, an (i, j)-path excluding F exists, i.e., D is strongly connected in G_F.

Algorithm 5.10 Equality (D)

1: Each process $i \in D$ sends t_i to all other processes in D along paths excluding F.
2: Each process $j \in D$ thus receives messages from all processes in D. Process j checks whether values received from all the processes in D and its own t_j are all equal, and also belong to $\{0, 1\}$. If these conditions are *not* satisfied, then $t_j := \bot$; otherwise t_j is not modified.

> ▷ For any process $k \notin D$, t_k is not modified in Equality(D). Also, for any process $k \in V$, v_k is not modified in Equality(D).

INNER Loop of Algorithm BC   Now we describe more details of the INNER loop. Particularly, we need to show that it is always possible to find such a set S given that $f > 0$ and G satisfies Condition BCS-G. For each F chosen in the OUTER loop, the INNER loop of Algorithm BC examines each partition A, B of $V \setminus F$ such that A, B are both non-empty. From Condition BCS-Prop and Corollary 5.15, we know that either $A \overset{V \setminus F}{\leadsto} B$ or $B \overset{V \setminus F}{\leadsto} A$. Therefore, with renaming of the sets we can ensure that $A \overset{V \setminus F}{\leadsto} B$. Then, depending on the choice of A, B, F, two cases may occur.

- Case 1 $A \overset{V \setminus F}{\leadsto} B$ and $B \overset{V \setminus F}{\not\leadsto} A$: We need to find a non-empty set $S \subseteq A$ such that $S \overset{V \setminus F}{\leadsto} V \setminus (F \cup S)$, and S is strongly connected in G_F.

- Case 2 $A \overset{V \setminus F}{\leadsto} B$ and $B \overset{V \setminus F}{\leadsto} A$: We need to find a non-empty set $S \subseteq A \cup B$ such that $S \overset{V \setminus F}{\leadsto} V \setminus (F \cup S)$, S is strongly connected in G_{-F}, and $A \overset{V \setminus F}{\leadsto} (S \setminus A)$.

The claim below ensures that Algorithm BC can be executed correctly in G in both cases. Here, we present a proof sketch, and the full proof is presented in [90].

Claim 5.1 *Suppose that $G = (V, E)$ satisfies Condition BCS-Prop. Then,*

- *the required set S exists in both Case 1 and 2 of each INNER loop, and*

- *each process in set F has enough incoming neighbors in $V \setminus F$ to perform step (j) of Algorithm BC with $f > 0$.*

Proof Sketch: It should be easy to make the following observation based on the definition of disjoint (A, b)-paths excluding F: *Given a partition A, B, F of V such that B is non-empty, and $|F| \leq f$, if $A \overset{V \setminus F}{\leadsto} B$, then size of A must be at least $f + 1$.*

Using this observation and Corollary 5.16, one can find the required set S. This proves the first claim.

For the second claim, note that Condition BCS-G implies that each process has at least $2f + 1$ incoming neighbors when $f > 0$. Now, consider processes in set F. Since $|F| \leq f$, for each $k \in F$ there must exist at least $f + 2$ incoming neighbors in $V \setminus F$. Thus, the desired set N_k exists, satisfying the requirement in step (j) of Algorithm BC.   □

Correctness of Algorithm BC

The correctness proof is based on the following two lemmas.

Lemma 5.17   *Suppose that $G = (V, E)$ satisfies Condition BCS-G. Then, for any $F \subset V$ and $F_1 \subset V \setminus F$, where $|F| \leq f$ and $|F_1| \leq f$, there exists a set of at least $f + 1$ processes $S \subseteq V \setminus F$ such that (i) processes in S are strongly connected in reduced graph G_{F,F_1}, and (ii) for each $j \in V \setminus (F \cup S)$, there exist at least $f + 1$ pairwise process-disjoint paths from S to j in G that do not contain any processes in F.*

Let v_j^{end} and v_j^{start} denote the value of v_j at the start and at the end of the INNER loop iteration, respectively. The following lemma ensures that the state at each fault-free process remains valid.

Lemma 5.18   *For any given INNER loop iteration, for each fault-free process $j \in V \setminus F^*$, there exists a fault-free process $s \in V \setminus F^*$ such that $v_j^{end} = v_j^{start}$.*

The proof of Lemma 5.17 is based on the definition of propagation, disjoint paths, reduced graphs, and Menger's Theorem. The proof of Lemma 5.18 is rather tedious, and proceeds by a careful step-by-step analysis of Algorithm BC. Both proofs can be found in [90].

Proof Intuition   Intuitively, the above $f + 1$ disjoint paths from the processes in S to processes in $V \setminus (F \cup S)$ provide adequate redundancy to allow propagation of values from the processes in S to the processes in $V \setminus (F \cup S)$, with the guarantee that any potential message tampering by faulty processes would not cause the recipients to accept an "invalid" value. In the fortuitous event that the processes in F are faulty and the processes in S (which are fault-free) have the same valid state variable, this value is then propagated to all the fault-free processes, achieving consensus. The algorithm ensures that this fortuitous event occurs at least once during the execution, particularly, when the processes in set F (chosen in each OUTER LOOP iteration) are all faulty, and thus the processes in set $S \subseteq V \setminus F$ are fault-free.

To prove that Algorithm BC is correct, we need to show that it achieves the validity, termination, and agreement properties.

Lemma 5.19   *Algorithm BC satisfies the validity property for Byzantine consensus.*

Proof.   Recall that the state v_i of a fault-free process i is *valid* if it equals the input at a fault-free process. For each fault-free $i \in V$, initially, v_i is valid. Lemma 5.18 implies that after each INNER loop iteration, v_i remains valid at each fault-free process i. Thus, when Algorithm BC terminates, v_i at each fault-free process i will satisfy the *validity* property.   □

Lemma 5.20   *Algorithm BC satisfies the termination property for Byzantine consensus.*

Proof. Recall that we assume a synchronous system, and the graph $G = (V, E)$ is finite. Thus, Algorithm BC performs a finite number of OUTER loop iterations, and a finite number of INNER loop iterations for each choice of F in the OUTER loop, the number of iterations being a function of graph $G = (V, E)$. Hence, the termination property is satisfied. □

Lemma 5.21   *Algorithm BC satisfies the agreement property for Byzantine consensus.*

Proof Sketch: The complete proof is presented in [90]. Recall that F^* denotes the actual set of faulty processes in G ($0 \leq |F^*| \leq f$). Since the OUTER loop considers all possible $F \subset V$ such that $|F| \leq f$, eventually, the OUTER loop will be performed with $F = F^*$. We will show that when OUTER loop is performed with $F = F^*$, *agreement* is achieved. After agreement is reached when $F = F^*$, Algorithm BC may perform the OUTER loop with other choices of set F. However, due to Lemma 5.18, the *agreement* among fault-free processes is still preserved. Moreover, due to Lemma 5.18, before the OUTER loop with $F = F^*$ is performed, v_i at each fault-free process remains valid.

Now, consider OUTER loop iteration with $F = F^*$. We will say that an INNER loop iteration with $F = F^*$ is "deciding" if one of the following conditions is true: (i) in Case 1 of the INNER loop iteration, after step (b) is performed, all the processes in set S have an identical value for variable $t \in \{0, 1\}$; or (ii) in Case 2 of the INNER loop iteration, after step (g) is performed, all the processes in set S have an identical value for variable $t \in \{0, 1\}$. As elaborated in [90], when $F = F^*$, at least one of the INNER loop iterations must be a *deciding* iteration. Let us partition the INNER loop iterations when $F = F^*$ into three phases.

- Phase 1: INNER loop iterations before the first deciding iteration with $F = F^*$.

- Phase 2: The first deciding iteration with $F = F^*$.

- Phase 3: Remaining INNER loop iterations with $F = F^*$.

From the pseudo-code for Propagate and Equality, observe that when $F = F^*$, all paths used in the INNER loop iterations *exclude* $F = F^*$. That is, all these paths contain only fault-free processes, since F^* is the actual set of faulty processes. In each INNER loop iteration in Phase 1, we can show that value v_i for each fault-free process i remains unchanged from previous INNER loop iteration. This together with fact that the value $v_i \in \{0, 1\}$ for each fault-free process i ensures that a *deciding* INNER loop iteration is eventually performed when $F = F^*$. In Phase 2, Algorithm BC achieves agreement among fault-free processes due to the fact that processes in set S reliably propagate an identical value to all the other processes. Finally, in Phase 3, due to Lemma 5.18, agreement achieved in the previous phase is preserved. Therefore, at the end of the OUTER loop with $F = F^*$, agreement is achieved. □

CHAPTER 6

Relay Depth and Approximate Consensus

In this chapter, we present results on the feasibility and efficiency of approximate consensus under different restrictions on the *relay depth*, i.e., the maximum number of hops that information (or a message) can be propagated (or relayed). This constraint is common in large-scale networks, and are used to avoid memory overload and network congestion, e.g., neighbor table and Time to live (TTL) (or hop limit) in the Internet Protocol.

To the best of our knowledge, Su and Vaidya [86] were the first to explore the Byzantine consensus problem under different relay depths in synchronous systems. Sakavalas, Tseng, and Vaidya [84] later extended the model to the *asynchronous* case, where they considered crash-tolerant consensus. Following the structure of the rest of the book, we will present the crash-tolerant result ([84]) first, followed by the Byzantine-tolerant result ([86]).

6.1 ITERATIVE k-HOP ALGORITHM

We are interested in a family of algorithms called iterative k-hop algorithms, where processes only have topology knowledge of their k-hop neighborhoods, and propagate state values to processes that are at most k-hops away. The results presented in this chapter also imply how k affects the *tight* conditions on the directed networks—lower k requires a more dense underlying communication network.

The iterative algorithms considered are a generalization of IAC, which have relay depth k and require each process i to perform the following three steps in *asynchronous* phase p.

1. *Transmit*: Transmit messages of the form $(v_i[p-1], p-1)$ to processes that are reachable from process i via at most k hops (including i), where $v_i[p-1]$ is the current state value. If process i is an intermediate process on the route of some message, then process i forwards that message as instructed by the source.

2. *Receive*: Receive messages from the processes that can reach process i via at most k hops (including i). Denote by $R_i[p]$ the set of messages that process i received at phase p.

3. *Update*: Update state using a transition function Z_i, where Z_i is a part of the specification of the algorithm, and takes as input the set $R_i[p]$, i.e.,

$$v_i[p] := Z_i(R_i[t]) = mean(R_i[t]).$$

The weighted mean function *mean* is as discussed in Section 1.4.1.

Note that (i) no exchange of topology information takes place in this class of algorithms, and (ii) each process' state only propagates within its k-hop neighborhood. For a process i, its k-hop incoming neighbors are defined as the processes j which are connected to i by a directed path in G that has $\leq k$ hops. The notion of k-hop outgoing neighbors is defined similarly. To tolerant Byzantine faults, one has to transmit a slightly more complicated messages which contain path information. We will discuss more details in Section 6.3.

Although in the distributed fault tolerance community, the notion of relay depth has not been largely considered, related notions appear in the distributed graph algorithms (DGA) community. Namely, it is an interesting open problem to examine the relation between the relay depth of an algorithm and the limitation of the maximum message size, as in the $\mathcal{CONGEST}$ model.

6.2   ASYNCHRONOUS CRASH FAULT TOLERANCE

We first explore the crash-tolerant approximate consensus problem in *asynchronous* incomplete networks under different restrictions on *relay depth* and *topology knowledge*—where we assume that each process knows all its neighbors of at most k-hop distance. The results on asynchronous crash-tolerant consensus have first been presented in [84]. The study presented in the following determines how topology knowledge and the relay depth affect the *tight* conditions on directed communication networks. Initially, we consider the case with k-hop topology knowledge and relay depth k for $1 \leq k \leq n$ and present a family of conditions, namely Condition k-CCA for $1 \leq k \leq n$, which prove to be necessary and sufficient for achieving asynchronous approximate consensus, through the use of iterative k-hop algorithms.

6.2.1   THE $k = 1$ CASE

One can observe that the special case of $k = 1$ coincides with the study of Section 4.2, where any process only transmits to its 1-hop neighbors. Thus, the tight Condition 1-CCA coincides with Condition CCA-I and algorithm LocWA presented in Section 4.2 proves its sufficiency. For completeness, we next state Condition 1-CCA, before we generalize it to the k-hop case.

Definition 6.1   (Condition 1-CCA $\equiv$ CCA-I).   For any partition L, C, R of V, where L and R are both non-empty, at least one of the following holds:

- $L \cup C \xrightarrow{f+1} R$

- $R \cup C \xrightarrow{f+1} L$

6.2.2 GENERAL k CASE

Now, consider the case when each process only knows its k-hop neighbors and the relay depth is k. In the following, we generalize the notions presented for the 1-hop case in above to the k-hop case. For process i, denote by $N_i^-(k)$ the set of i's k-hop incoming neighbors, For a set of processes A, let N_A^- be the set of A's one-hop incoming neighbors. Formally, $N_A^- = \{i \mid i \in V \setminus A, \text{ and } \exists j \in A, (i, j) \in E\}$. Next, we define the generalization of the $A \xrightarrow{f+1} B$ relation for the k-hop case; for convenience we will simply denote it with $A \to_k B$.

Definition 6.2 $A \to_k B$. Given disjoint non-empty subsets of processes-nodes A and B, we will say that $A \to_k B$ holds if there exists a node i in B for which there exist at least $f + 1$ node-disjoint paths of length at most k from distinct nodes in A to i. More formally, if $\mathcal{P}_i^A(k)$ is the family of all sets of node-disjoint paths (with i being their only common node) of length at most k, initiating in A and ending in node i, $A \to_k B$ means that $\exists i \in B, \max_{P \in \mathcal{P}_i^A(k)} |P| \geq f + 1$.

Definition 6.3 **Condition k-CCA.** For any partition L, C, R of V, where L and R are both non-empty, either $L \cup C \to_k R$ or $R \cup C \to_k L$.

The necessity of Condition k-CCA for achieving asynchronous approximate consensus through an iterative k-hop algorithm holds analogously with the one-hop case (Section 4.2.1), where a set of x incoming neighbors of process i has to be replaced with a set of x distinct processes that reach i through disjoint paths. For sufficiency, we next present a generalization of Algorithm LocWA for the k-hop case in Algorithm 6.11. There are two differences between Algorithm 6.11 k-LocWA and LocWA, are the following:

- processes transmit its state to all their k-hop outgoing neighbors, and

- Algorithm k-LocWA relies on the generalized version of Condition 1-WAIT, presented below.

Definition 6.4 **Condition k-WAIT.** For $F_i \subseteq N_i^-(k)$, we denote with $reach_i^k(F_i)$ the set of processes that have paths of length $l \leq k$ to process i in $G_{V \setminus F_i}$. That is, the set of k-hop incoming neighbors of i that remain connected with i even when all processes in set F_i crash. The condition is satisfied at process i, in phase p if there exists $F_i \subseteq N_i^-(k)$ with $|F_i[p]| \leq f$ such that $reach_i^k(F_i[p]) \subseteq heard_i[p]$.

We present Algorithm 6.11 k-LocWA, which utilizes Condition k-WAIT. For brevity, we do not specify how the network routes the messages within the k-hop neighborhood of each process—this can be achieved by using local flooding through tagging a hop counter in each message (cf. line 4 of Algorithm 6.11).

Algorithm 6.11 k-LocWA (Local-Wait-Average)

===

(For process $i \in V$)
Initialization: $v_i[0] :=$ input of node i
Constant: p_{end} (Defined in Equation 6.1)

1: **for** phase $p := 1$ **to** p_{end} **do**
2:     $R_i[p] := \{v_i[p-1]\}$
3:     $heard_i[p] := \{i\}$
4:     Send message $(v_i[p-1], i, p)$ to processes in $N_i^+(k)$, i.e., all k-hop outgoing neighbors
5:     **repeat**
6:         **if** message (h, j, p) is received for the *first time*, **then**
7:             $R_i[p] := R_i[p] \cup \{h\}$ $\triangleright$ $R_i[p]$ is a multiset
8:             $heard_i[p] := heard_i[p] \cup \{j\}$
9:         **end if**
10:     **until** Condition k-WAIT is satisfied
11:     Update state as:

$$v_i[p] := \frac{\sum_{v \in R_i[p]} v}{|R_i[p]|}$$

12: **end for**
13: **output** $v_i[p]$

===

For simplicity, we assume that the input at each process is some *real number* in the range $[0, K]$, where $K \in \mathbb{R}$ is known *a priori*. To argue about the termination of k-LocWA, in the following, we assume that p_{end} is any integer with

$$p_{end} > \frac{(n-f-1)\log(\epsilon/K)}{\log\left(1 - \frac{\alpha_k^{n-f-1}}{2}\right)}, \tag{6.1}$$

where $\alpha_k = \min_{i \in V} \frac{1}{|N_i^-(k)|}$. Since we typically want ϵ to be small, we naturally assume that $\epsilon < K$. The rigorous termination study can be found in [84].

Correctness of Algorithm k-LocWA

Proving the correctness of Algorithm k-LocWA follows a similar reasoning of the correctness of LocWA as presented in Section 4.2.2. The key here is to identify Condition k-CCA and Condition k-WAIT so that the proof structure remains almost identical. To adapt the arguments to the general case, one should define the analogous $in(A \rightarrow_k B)$ definition based on the general $A \rightarrow_k B$ notion of Definition 4.5.

Definition 6.5   For disjoint sets A, B, $in(A \rightarrow_k B)$ denotes the set of all the processes i in B that there exist least $f + 1$ incoming disjoint paths of length at most k from distinct processes in $N_i^- \cap A$ to i. When $A \nrightarrow_k B$, define $in(A \rightarrow_k B) = \emptyset$. Formally, in terminology of Definition 6.2: $in(A \rightarrow B) = \{i \in B : \max\{|P| : \max_{P \in \mathcal{P}_i^A(k)} |P| \geq f + 1\}$

The correctness proof of Algorithm k-LocWA is similar to the proof of Theorem 4.9; remarks on the arguments' adaptations are presented in the proof sketch of the following theorem.

Theorem 6.6   *Approximate crash-tolerant consensus in an asynchronous system using iterative k-hop algorithms is feasible iff G satisfies Condition k-CCA.*

Proof Sketch: Having defined the basic notion $in(A \rightarrow_k B)$, Definition 4.6 of the notion A *propagates to B* is the same for the k-hop case. Intuitively, if A *propagates to B*, information will be propagated gradually from A to B in l steps; corruption of any faulty set of f processes will *not* be able to block propagation to a specific process i because the definition of $in(A \rightarrow_k B)$ guarantees that i will receive information from at least $f + 1$ disjoint paths if it has not crashed. A difference with the original case is that for every of the l steps needed to propagate from A to B, k communication steps will be required in the worst case, since information may be propagated through paths of length k. Lemma 4.8 is intuitively the same since it is based on the general propagation notion but value α which is defined based on the number of incoming neighbors will now be defined on the number of k-hop incoming neighbors, i.e., $\alpha_k = \min_{i \in V} \frac{1}{|N_i^-(k)|}$. The main correctness proof remains essentially the same since it repeatedly makes use of the abstract propagation notion between various sets, without focusing on how the values are propagated. $\square$

6.2.3   CONDITION RELATION

We first compare the feasibility of approximate consensus for different values of k by presenting a relation among the various k-CCA conditions as well as their relation with Condition CCA-G (Definition 2.10). Intuitively, achieving approximate consensus for a lower k requires the existence of more paths in the graph; this can be observed by definition and is summarized in the following theorem.

Theorem 6.7   *For values $k, k' \in \mathbb{N}$ with $k \leq k'$, Condition k-CCA implies Condition k'-CCA.*

Proof. Let Condition k-CCA hold and assume, without loss of generality that $L \cup C \rightarrow_k R$ holds for a partition L, C, R. This means that there exists a process i in R that has at least $f + 1$ incoming disjoint paths of length at most k initiating from distinct processes in $L \cup C$.

Consequently, the same $f + 1$ paths will consist i's incoming disjoint paths of length at most k', since $k' \geq k$, and thus, $L \cup C \to_{k'} R$ which means that k'-CCA holds. $\square$

We next show that Condition CCA-G is equivalent to Condition n-CCA. The proof illustrates how the locally defined Condition k-CCA naturally coincides with the globally defined Condition CCA-G in the extreme case.

Theorem 6.8   *Condition CCA-G is equivalent to Condition n-CCA.*

Proof. It is easy to see that Condition n-CCA implies Condition CCA. If Condition CCA-G is violated in G, then Condition n-CCA does not hold either, since L and R have at most f one-hop incoming neighbors.

Now, we show the other direction. Assume for the sake of contradiction that Condition CCA-G holds but Condition n-CCA does not. Then, there exists a partition L, C, R with $L, R \neq \emptyset$ such that $L \cup C \not\to_k R$ and $R \cup C \not\to_k L$. Since Condition CCA-G holds, we have that either $L \cup C \overset{f+1}{\rightarrowtail} R$ or $R \cup C \overset{f+1}{\rightarrowtail} L$. Now consider the case that $L \cup C \overset{f+1}{\rightarrowtail} R$ and $R \cup C \overset{f+1}{\not\rightarrowtail} L$. This means that $|N_R^-| \geq f + 1$ and $|N_L^-| \leq f$. The case of $L \cup C \overset{f+1}{\not\rightarrowtail} R$ and $R \cup C \overset{f+1}{\rightarrowtail} L$ is symmetrical and the case of $L \cup C \overset{f+1}{\rightarrowtail} R$ and $R \cup C \overset{f+1}{\rightarrowtail} L$ can be proved by applying the argument below once for set R and once for set L.

Let i be the process in R with the maximum number m of disjoint paths initiating from distinct processes in $V \setminus R$ (as implied by Definition 6.2). The fact $L \cup C \not\to_k R$ implies that $m \leq f$. Subsequently, $|N_R^-| \geq f + 1$ implies that the set $A = N_R^- - N_i^-(n)$ is non-empty (the maximal subset of N_R^- which does not contain any n-hop incoming neighbors of i). Let $B = N_A^+(n) \cap R$ be the set of all the outgoing n-hop neighbors of all processes $j \in A$ confined in the set R. By definition of B and A, it holds that $N_i^-(n) \cap B = \emptyset$. We can now create a new partition $L' = L, C' = C \cup B, R' = R - B$ by moving B from R to C. For partition L', C', R' it holds that $L', R' \neq \emptyset$ since $i \in R'$ and $L' = L$. Moreover, it holds that (i) $|N_{R'}^-| \leq f$, since $|N_{R'}^-| = |N_R^- - A|$ and $A \neq \emptyset$; and (ii) $|N_L^-| \leq f$ since $L = L'$. The latter points imply that $R \cup C \overset{f+1}{\not\rightarrow} L$ and $L \cup C \overset{f+1}{\not\rightarrow} R$, which yield a contradiction to the hypothesis that Condition CCA-G holds. This completes the proof. $\square$

6.2.4   TOPOLOGY DISCOVERY AND UNLIMITED RELAY DEPTH

Here, we consider the case of one-hop topology knowledge and relay depth n. In other words, processes initially only know their immediate incoming and outgoing neighbors, but processes can flood the network and learn the topology. The study of this case is motivated by the observation that full topology knowledge at each process requires a much higher deployment and configuration cost. We show that Condition CCA-G is necessary and sufficient for solving approximate consensus with one-hop neighborhood knowledge and relay depth n in asynchronous directed networks. Compared to the iterative k-hop algorithms in Section 6.2, the algorithms considered here are *not* restricted in the sense that processes can propagate any messages to all the reachable processes.

The necessity of Condition CCA-G is implied by Theorem 4.10. The algorithms presented below are again inspired by Algorithm WA from [93]. The main contribution is to show how each process can learn "enough" topology information to solve approximate consensus—this technique may be of interests in other contexts as well. In the discussion below, we present an algorithm that works in any directed graph that satisfies Condition CCA.

Algorithm LWA   The idea of Algorithm 6.12 LWA (Learn-Wait-Average) is to piggyback the information of incoming neighbors when propagating state values. Then, each process i will locally construct an *estimated* graph $G^i[p]$ in every phase p, and check whether Condition n-WAIT holds in $G^i[p]$ or not. Note that $G^i[p]$ may not equal to G, as process i may not receive messages from some other processes due to asynchrony or failures. The termination of the algorithm can be guaranteed with its slight modification in a way similar to [28, 58]. To facilitate the presentation of the algorithm we use the notion of "union of graphs" in line 9 of Algorithm 6.12, i.e, if $G_1 = (V_1, E_1)$ and $G_2(V_2, E_2)$ then $G_1 \cup G_2 \equiv G_3(V_3, E_3)$, where $V_3 = V_1 \cup V_2$ and $E_3 = E_1 \cup E_2$. Note that this is *not* a multiset, there is only one copy of each process or edge.

We say Condition n-WAIT holds in the local estimated graph $G^i[p] = (V^i[p], E^i[p])$ if **there exists** a set $F_i[p] \subseteq V^i[p] - \{i\}$, where $|F_i[p]| \leq f$, such that $reach'_i(F_i[p]) \subseteq heard_i[p]$. Here, $reach'_i(F_i)$ is the set of processes that have paths to process i in the subgraph induced by the processes in $V^i[p] - F_i[p]$ for $F_i[p] \subseteq V^i[p] - \{i\}$ and $|F_i[p]| \leq f$.

Recall that N_i^- denotes the set of i's one-hop incoming neighbors. Given a set of processes N and process i, we also use the notation $G_{N \Rightarrow i}$ to describe a directed graph consisting of processes $N \cup \{i\}$ and set of directed edges from each process in N to i. Formally, $G_{N \Rightarrow i} = (N \cup \{i\}, E')$, where $E' = \{(j, i) \mid j \in N\}$.

Correctness of Algorithm LWA

The key lemma to prove the correctness of Algorithm WA is to show that for any pair of processes that have not crashed in phase p, they must receive a state value from at least one common process. In the following, we show that Algorithm LWA achieves the same property. Intuitively, if Condition n-WAIT does not hold in the local estimated graph $G^i[p]$, then process i knows it can learn more states in phase p. Also, when Condition n-WAIT is satisfied in $G^i[p]$, there exists a scenario that process i cannot receive any more information; hence, it should not wait for any more message. This is why the Algorithm LWA allows each process to learn enough state values to achieve approximate consensus. We next rely on this observation to prove the correctness.

We assume that the graph $G = (V, E)$ satisfies Condition CCA. In a given execution of Algorithm LWA, define $F[p]$ as the processes i that have *not* computed value $v_i[p]$ for a

---

Algorithm 6.12 LWA (Learn-Wait-Average)

(For process $i \in V$)
Initialization:
$v_i[0] :=$ input of node i
$G^i[0] := G_{N_i^- \Rightarrow i}$

1: **for** phase $p \geq 1$ **do**
2:    $R_i[p] := \{v_i[p-1]\}$
3:    $heard_i[p] := \{i\}$
4:    Send message $(v_i[p-1], N_i^-, i, p)$ to all the outgoing neighbors
5:    **repeat**
6:       **if** message (h, Nj, p) is received for the *first time*, **then**
7:          $R_i[p] := R_i[p] \cup \{h\}$ ▷ $R_i[p]$ is a multiset
8:          $heard_i[p] := heard_i[p] \cup \{j\}$
9:          $G^i[p] := G^i[p] \cup G_{N \Rightarrow j}$
10:         Send message (h, N, j, p) to all the outgoing neighbors
11:      **end if**
12:   **until** Condition n-WAIT is satisfied on $G^i[p]$
13:   Update state as:
$$v_i[p] := \frac{\sum_{v \in R_i[p]} v}{|R_i[p]|}$$

14:   $G^i[p+1] := G_{N_i^- \Rightarrow i}$ ▷ "Reset" the learned graph
15: **end for**

---

fixed phase p. In the discussion below, we will drop the phase index p for some notation for brevity. Results in [93] implies that Condition WAIT must hold at some point on the local estimated graph G^i, e.g., when process i receives every message. Since G^i is evolving as process i receives more messages. Suppose Condition WAIT holds on $G^{i*} = (V^{i*}, E^{i*})$ for the first time at process i. At that point of time, let $heard_i^*[p]$, $R_i^*[p]$ denote the set $heard_i[p]$ and the corresponding multiset $R_i[p]$. The following lemma is the main argument for the correctness of Algorithm LWA. The proof is similar to the one for Algorithm WA, hence it is omitted.

Lemma 6.9 *Fix a phase $p \geq 1$. For any pair of processes $i, j \in V \setminus F[p]$, $heard_i^*[p] \cap heard_j^*[p] \neq \emptyset$.*

Similar to the proofs in [58, 93], the lemma together with simple algebra, it is easy to show that Algorithm LWA achieves Validity and Convergence.

Undirected Graphs

Algorithm LWA works on undirected graphs as well; however, the message size is large, since each message needs to include the information about one's neighborhood. In [85], an algorithm is presented where each process learns the topology in the first phase, and then executes an approximate consensus algorithm using the learned topology. The reasons that this trick *only* works in undirected graphs are: (i) Condition CCA-G is equivalent to $(f + 1)$ connectivity and $n > 2f$ in undirected graph; and (ii) for each process, there is at least one fault-free neighbor; hence, each process is able to learn the existence of every other process.

6.3   SYNCHRONOUS BYZANTINE FAULT TOLERANCE

As mentioned previously, Su and Vaidya [86] were the first to study Byzantine fault-tolerance under different relay depths. In the discussion below, we present results from [86], in which the authors determine the tight topological condition under which approximate consensus is possible using iterative k-hop algorithm in a synchronous system with Byzantine faults. The relay depth and topology knowledge is assumed to be identical in [86]. That is, each process knows its k-hop neighborhood and each message is propagated to at most k hops away. An interesting related open problem is the study of topology discovery in the presence of Byzantine faults under this setting.

6.3.1   CONDITION BCS-k

We first introduce several concepts to define Condition BCS-k which was proved to be both necessary and sufficient in [86]. Intuitively, Condition BCS-k requires that either the set of processes in $R \cup C$ are able to "collectively influence" the state of some process in L using paths that are at most k hops or vice versa. Note that when $k = 1$, it should be easy to observe that Condition BCS-k is equivalent to Condition BCS-I. In [86], it was shown that Condition BCS-n is equivalent to Condition BCS-G.

Recall that the notion of reduced graph was introduced in Section 5.2. The condition uses the notion $A \rightarrow_k B$, defined in Definition 6.2.

Definition 6.10   Condition k-BCS.   For any process partition L, C, R, F of V such that $L \neq \emptyset, R \neq \emptyset$ and $|F| \leq f$, in the reduced G_F, at least one of the two conditions below must be true: (i) $R \cup C \rightarrow_k L$; (ii) $L \cup C \rightarrow_k R$.

6.3.2   NECESSITY AND SUFFICIENCY

Here, we briefly discuss why Condition k-BCS is tight.

Necessity Proof   The necessity proof in [86] is similar to the one for Condition BCS-I. The structure is as follows: suppose by way of contradiction that there exists a correct iterative k-hop algorithm, then similar to the proof of Condition BCS-I, we can find a process partition violating Condition k-BCS. More precisely, we can construct a scenario such that under certain Byzantine faulty behavior of processes in F, and for some specific initial inputs, the correctness properties will be violated.

Sufficiency   Unlike in crash-tolerant case, each process i may receive bogus or tampered messages due to the existence of Byzantine processes. To address the issue, Su and Vaidya [86] rely on two mechanisms: (i) attaching the path information to each message (i.e., source routing) and (ii) trimming some values from the received messages $R_i[p]$ during the update step using a notion of "message cover."

   The message used in the algorithm is in the form of a tuple $m = (w, P)$, where $w \in \mathbb{R}$ is the state value and P indicates the path via which message m should be transmitted. Four functions are defined over the message m sent from process i to process j using path P:

- value$(m) = w$

- path$(m) = P$

- source$(m) = i$

- destination$(m) = j$

   Fix a process. Let $\mathcal{M}$ be a set of messages received in the second step of the Synchronous IAC algorithm, and $\mathcal{P}(\mathcal{M})$ the set of paths from which the processes received the messages in $\mathcal{M}$, i.e., $\mathcal{P}(\mathcal{M}) = \{\text{path}(m) | m \in \mathcal{M}\}$.

Definition 6.11   Message Cover.   A message cover of $\mathcal{M}$ is a set of processes $\mathcal{T}(\mathcal{M}) \subseteq \mathcal{V}(G)$, such that for each path $P \in \mathcal{P}$

$$\mathcal{V}(P) \cap \mathcal{T}(\mathcal{M}) \neq \emptyset.$$

Definition 6.12   Minimum Message Cover.   A minimum message cover is defined by

$$\mathcal{T}^*(\mathcal{M}) \in \underset{\mathcal{T}(\mathcal{M}) \subseteq \mathcal{V}(G):\ \mathcal{T}(\mathcal{M})\ \text{is a cover of}\ \mathcal{M}}{\text{argmin}} |\mathcal{T}(\mathcal{M})|.$$

Definition 6.13   Given a set of messages $\mathcal{M}_0$ and a set of processes $\mathcal{T} \subseteq \mathcal{V}(G)$, a maximal set of messages $\mathcal{M} \subseteq \mathcal{M}_0$ that are covered by $\mathcal{T}$ is defined by

$$\mathcal{M}^* \in \underset{\mathcal{M} \subseteq \mathcal{M}_0:\ \mathcal{T}\ \text{is a cover of}\ \mathcal{M}}{\text{argmax}} |\mathcal{M}|.$$

Let $\mathcal{M}_i$ be the set of messages received by a process i at some phase. Then, we define a procedure *Trim* in Algorithm 6.13. Note that in Algorithm Trim, subscripts "s", "l" in lines 2,3 stand for smaller and larger, respectively.

Algorithm 6.13 Trim($\mathcal{M}_i$)

Initialization: $\mathcal{M}'_i := \mathcal{M}_i \setminus \{(v_i[t-1], (i,i))\}$.

1: Sort messages in $\mathcal{M}'_i$ in an increasing order, according to their message fields, i.e., value(m) for $m \in \mathcal{M}'_i$.
2: Let $\mathcal{M}_{is} \subseteq \mathcal{M}'_i$ such that (i) for all $m \in \mathcal{M}'_i \setminus \mathcal{M}_{is}$ and $m' \in \mathcal{M}_{is}$ we have value(m) $\geq$ value(m'); and (ii) the cardinality of a minimum cover of $\mathcal{M}_{is}$ is exactly f, i.e., $|\mathcal{T}^*(\mathcal{M}_{is})| = f$.
3: Let $\mathcal{M}_{il} \subseteq \mathcal{M}'_i$ such that (i) for all $m \in \mathcal{M}'_i \setminus \mathcal{M}_{il}$ and $m'' \in \mathcal{M}_{il}$ we have value(m) $\leq$ value(m''); and (ii) the cardinality of a minimum cover of $\mathcal{M}_{il}$ is exactly f, i.e., $|\mathcal{T}^*(\mathcal{M}_{il})| = f$.
4: Return $\mathcal{M}'_i \setminus (\mathcal{M}_{is} \cup \mathcal{M}_{il})$.

Theorem 6.14   *Suppose that the graph G satisfies Condition k-BCS, then $\mathcal{M}^*_i$ is non-empty.*

This theorem is proved by construction, i.e., an algorithm is constructed to find the sets $\mathcal{M}_{is}, \mathcal{M}_{il}$ for a given $\mathcal{M}'_i$ such that $\mathcal{M}_{is}[t], \mathcal{M}_{il}[t]$ are well defined and $\mathcal{M}'_i$ contains at least one more element than $\mathcal{M}_{is} \cup \mathcal{M}_{il}$. Please refer to [86] for more details.

The iterative k-hop algorithm from [86] is presented in Algorithm 6.14 below. By construction, we have $\mathcal{M}^*_i[p] = \mathcal{M}'_i[p] \setminus (\mathcal{M}_{is}[p] \cup \mathcal{M}_{il})[p]$. The "weight" of each term on the right-hand side of (6.2) is a_i, where $0 < a_i \leq 1$, and these weights add to 1.

In Algorithm 6.14 ISB (*Iterative-Synchronous-Byzantine*), each fault-free process i's state, $v_i[p]$, is updated as a convex combination of all the *messages values* collected by process i at phase p. In particular, for each message $m \in \mathcal{M}'[p]$, its coefficient is a_i if the message is in $\mathcal{M}^*_i[p]$ or the message is sent via self-loop of process i; otherwise, the coefficient of m is zero. Note that with multi-hop communication, fault-free process can possibly receive messages via multiple routes. The **Trim** function takes the possible multi-route messages into account. In fact, Algorithm 6.14 also works with multi-graphs.

The correctness can be argued using a similar propagation-based argument in Theorem 6.6 and the observation that all the extreme values will be discarded by the *Trim* function. Su and Vaidya [86] used an alternative approach that proves correctness succinctly. They first construct a matrix form to represent the state evolution of fault-free processes using Algorithm 6.14. Validity follows directly from the observation that states can be derived by computing the product of row-stochastic matrices. Then they use toolkit of weak-ergodic theory to show convergence.

Algorithm 6.14 ISB (Iterative-Synchronous-Byzantine)

(For process $i \in V$)
Initialization: $v_i[0] :=$ input of node i

1: *Transmit step:* Transmit messages of the form $(v_i[t - 1], \cdot)$ to processes in $N_i^+(k)$. If process i is an intermediate process of some message, then process i forwards that message as instructed by the message's path field.

2: *Receive step:* Receive messages from $N_i^-(k)$. When process i expects to receive a message from a path but does not receive the message, the message value is assumed to be equal to some default message. Let $\mathcal{M}_i[p]$ be the set of messages received.

3: *Update step:* Let $\mathcal{M}_i^*[p] = Trim(\mathcal{M}_i[p])$. Then define

$$v_i[p] = a_i v_i[t - 1] + \sum_{m \in \mathcal{M}_i^*[p]} a_i w_m, \tag{6.2}$$

where $w_m = \mathsf{value}(m)$ and $a_i = \frac{1}{|\mathcal{M}_i^*[p]|+1}$.

One novelty is the notion of message cover and the accompanied *Trim* function, which allows the construction of a matrix form of nice properties.

PART III

Other Adversarial Models

CHAPTER 7

Broadcast Under Local Adversaries

In the rest of the book, we will present topological conditions that have appeared in the literature and affect consensus feasibility in different settings than the ones addressed up to this point. We will consider different adversary models and level of topology knowledge as well as more fundamental reliable communication problems, the feasibility of which naturally affects consensus solvability. All results presented are studied in the context of the *synchronous* message-passing model.

In this chapter, we will focus on the *reliable broadcast* problem where the goal is to have some designated process, called the *sender*, reliably send its input value to all other processes in the network. The problem was introduced in [50] as the *Byzantine Generals* problem. Unlike the general case where the sender may also be corrupted, we will focus on the case when the sender is fault-free. The latter problem is already non-trivial in incomplete networks and we will simply call it *broadcast*. The more descriptive name of *one-to-all* reliable message transmission has been also used in the literature for this special case.

Intuitively, the difficulty introduced by the incomplete network topology can be captured by the simple case of a fault-free sender. To argue about this, one has to observe that for the Byzantine Generals problem, as well as for the equivalent consensus problem (i.e., Byzantine-tolerant Consensus or *Byzantine Agreement*[1]), many protocols for complete networks appearing in the literature utilize one-to-all message transmission in each round. Therefore, one can obtain solutions for the incomplete network case by using a broadcast subroutine to simulate one-to-all reliable transmission from every process. Naturally, the resulting protocol will solve the problem under the correctness assumptions of the given complete network protocol. Specifically, the weakest sufficient condition for the existence of a Byzantine Generals and consensus protocol is determined by the classic impossibility bound of [50], which additionally has to hold for the correctness of the solution; the latter states that the overall number of corruptions must be smaller that $n/3$. This means that a sufficient topological condition for broadcast, considering any process as sender, also implies a sufficient condition for consensus and Byzantine Generals to be feasible; the argument is formalized in Corollary 7.12.

The presented results concern the *local adversary model* introduced by Koo [45] (cf. Section 1.2.1). A local adversary is restricted to corrupt up to a fixed number f of corruptions in

---

[1]Byzantine Agreement is trivially equivalent to Byzantine Generals under polynomial computations.

the neighborhood of any node in the graph; intuitively, the corruptions can be considered to be distributed evenly across the graph. A line of research (e.g., [41, 56, 73, 79, 89]) summarized in this chapter has considered *ad hoc* incomplete networks, where the topology knowledge of the processes is restricted to their own neighborhood. The importance of the local adversary model comes, among others, from the fact that local adversary restrictions may be used to derive local criteria which can be employed in *ad hoc* networks. We will mainly focus on the results pertinent to undirected networks; extensions to the directed network case are outlined in Section 7.5.2.

7.1 PRELIMINARIES AND TOPOLOGICAL CONDITIONS

Below we formally define the fault-free sender reliable broadcast problem which will be referred in the following simply as *broadcast*.

Definition 7.1 Reliable Broadcast with a Fault-Free Sender (Broadcast). We assume the existence of a designated process $s \in V$, called the *sender*, which has initial input value x_s. We say that a distributed protocol Π achieves (or solves) broadcast in (G, s), if all fault-free processes eventually decide on the value x_s, i.e., they output the sender's initial input value value.

Regarding the topology knowledge of the processes, we will consider the *ad hoc* network model (cf. [79]), where each process is only aware of its own id, the id's of its immediate neighbors, and the id of the sender. The results presented are pertinent to the *local adversary model* (also referred to as the locally bounded adversary model) where the adversary can corrupt at most $f \in \mathbb{N}$ processes in the neighborhood N_i of each process $i \in V$. The family of f-*local* sets (defined below) plays an important role in our study since it coincides with the family of admissible corruption sets.

Definition 7.2 f-local set. Given a graph $G = (V, E)$ and a $f \in \mathbb{N}$ a f-*local set* is a set $C \subseteq V$ for which $\forall i \in V, |N_i \cap C| \leq f$. For $V' \subseteq V$ a f-*local w.r.t. V' set* is a set $C \subseteq V$ for which $\forall i \in V', |N_i \cap C| \leq f$.

In the following, we will often make use of node-cuts which separate some processes from the sender, i.e., node-cuts that do not include the sender. From here on we will simply use the term *cut* to denote such a node-cut. The notion of f-*local pair cut* was introduced in [79] and its non-existence was proved in [73] to be a tight condition for broadcast in known topology graphs.

Definition 7.3 f-local pair cut. Given a graph $G = (V, E)$ and $f \in \mathbb{N}$, a pair of f-local sets C_1, C_2 s.t. $C_1 \cup C_2$ is a cut of G is called a f-*local pair cut*.

The next definition extends the notion of f-local pair cut and is particularly useful in describing capability of achieving broadcast in *ad hoc* networks where each process' knowledge of the topology is limited in its own neighborhood.

Definition 7.4 f-partial local pair cut.   Let C be a cut of G, partitioning $V \setminus C$ into sets $A, B \neq \emptyset$ s.t. $s \in A$. C is a *f-partial local pair cut (f-plp cut)* if there exists a partition $C = C_1 \cup C_2$ where C_1 is f-local and C_2 is f-local w.r.t. B.

Definition 7.5   Condition PLC.   For a graph G and sender node s, we will denote the *non-*existence of an f-plp cut with Condition PLC (Partial-Local-cut).

As we will see in the following, proving the feasibility of broadcast in *ad hoc* networks may include arguments for graphs different from G where the execution is considered; this happens because the whole topology of the graph is unknown to the processes and thus, their decision must cover all topology cases. For this reason we define the following notion which is instance-specific, i.e., it depends on the graph-sender pair (G, s).

Definition 7.6 f-locally resilient algorithm for (G, s).   An algorithm which achieves broadcast in a given graph G with sender s for any f-local corruption set F and any behavior of F is called *f-locally resilient* for (G, s).

In the course of this chapter, we consider the natural class of *safe* broadcast algorithms, i.e., algorithms that never cause a process to decide on an incorrect value. The importance of the safety property is pointed out in [79], where it is regarded as a basic requirement of a broadcast algorithm. Essentially, a safe broadcast algorithm ensures that a process i will decide on a value v only in the case that i can undoubtedly deduce from its view (input and exchanged messages) that the value v is the actual input value of the sender.

Definition 7.7   Safe/ f-locally safe algorithm.   An algorithm which never causes a fault-free process to decide on (output) an incorrect value, for any graph-sender pair (G, s) under any corruption set and any behavior of it (that is, given any adversary model), is called *safe*.
An algorithm which never causes a fault-free process to decide on an incorrect value under any f-local corruption set and any behavior of it, for any graph-sender pair (G, s), is called *f-locally safe*.

Resilient vs. Safe Algorithms   Observe that in a system executing an f-locally resilient algorithm, there is a case that the processes will output incorrect values in an instance that broadcast is impossible. The notion of a safe algorithm implies the additional property that even in an instance where broadcast is impossible, the processes will either output the correct value (sender's value) or will not output anything. Namely, a safe algorithm might still fail, particularly by not correctly delivering the message to all processes of the network. By not correctly we mean that the information received by a process is not sufficient for it to decide. Essentially, a safe broadcast algorithm ensures that a process will decide on a value only in the case it can undoubtedly deduce from its view (input and exchanged messages) that this is the actual value of the sender.

In the following section, the necessity of condition PLC for achieving *ad hoc* broadcast in the class of safe algorithms will be presented.

7.2 NECESSITY OF CONDITION PLC FOR *AD HOC* BROADCAST

Condition PLC was shown in [73] to be necessary for the existence of a f-locally safe broadcast algorithm in *ad hoc* networks. We will call an algorithm that operates under the *ad hoc* knowledge assumptions an *ad hoc broadcast algorithm*.

Theorem 7.8 Necessary Condition. *Let $\mathcal{A}$ be a f-locally safe ad hoc broadcast algorithm. Given a graph G, a bound $f \in \mathbb{N}$ and a sender s, if condition PLC does not hold in (G, s), then $\mathcal{A}$ is not f-locally resilient in (G, s).*

Proof. Since PLC is not satisfied, we can assume the partition of set V in the sets A, B, F, H such that $C = F \cup H$ is a f-plp cut in graph G with sender s which disconnects the process sets A, B. Let F be the f-local set of the cut partition and H the f-local w.r.t. to B set (Figure 7.1). Let G' be a graph that results from G if we remove some edges that connect processes in $A \cup F \cup H$ with processes in H so that the set H becomes f-local in G' (e.g., we can remove all edges that connect processes in $A \cup F \cup H$ with processes in H). Note that the existence of a set of edges that guarantees such a property is implied by the fact that H is f-local w.r.t. B.

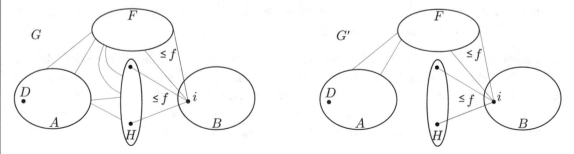

Figure 7.1: Indistinguishable graphs G and G' in the *ad hoc* model.

The proof is by contradiction. Suppose that there exists a f-locally safe broadcast algorithm $\mathcal{A}$ which is f-locally resilient in graph G with sender s. We consider the following executions σ and σ' of $\mathcal{A}$.

- Execution σ is on the graph G with sender s, with sender's value $x_s = 0$, and corruption set F; in each round, each corrupted process in F performs the actions that its corresponding process performs in the respective round of execution σ' (where F is a set of fault-free processes).

- Execution σ' is on the graph G' with sender s, with sender's value $x_s = 1$, and corruption set H; in each round, each corrupted process in H performs the actions that its corresponding process performs in the respective round of execution σ (where H is a set of fault-free processes).

Although the above definitions of σ, σ' may seem circular, in fact the actions of processes are well defined as is explained in the note after the proof. Note that F, H are admissible corruption sets in G, G', respectively, due to their f-locality. It is easy to see that $H \cup F$ is a cut which separates s from B in both G and G' and that actions of every process of this cut are identical in both executions σ, σ'. Consequently, the actions of any fault-free process $i \in B$ must be identical in both executions. Since, by assumption, algorithm $\mathcal{A}$ is f-locally resilient on G with sender s, i must decide on the sender's message 0 in execution σ on G with sender s, and must do the same in execution σ' on G' with sender s. However, in execution σ' the sender's message is 1. Therefore, $\mathcal{A}$ makes i decide on an incorrect message in (G', s). This contradicts the assumption that $\mathcal{A}$ is locally safe. □

Note on the proof of Theorem 7.8. Although the argument of the two simultaneous executions σ, σ' is standard in the literature (e.g., [26, 45, 46, 79]), it may seem that the definition of the actions of the corrupted processes is circular and thus are not well defined. For ease of presentation we denote with F, H the sets of the execution σ and with F', H' their respective sets in the execution σ'. The circularity of the definition may (falsely) appear in the following example; the actions of F depend on the actions of F' which may in turn depend on the messages they receive from H' which depend on the actions of H in σ which may lastly depend on the actions of F in the same execution. To overcome this obstacle we observe that the actions of all processes are uniquely defined in an inductive manner, i.e., in the first round of both executions the actions of fault-free processes in the sets H, F' are uniquely defined by the deterministic protocol $\mathcal{A}$ and their initial values due to the fact that no messages have been received. Therefore, the actions of the first round that the respective corruption sets H', F take are uniquely defined by the actions of H, F'. Assuming that the actions (exchanged messages) of all processes are uniquely defined until the end of round k, one can observe that the actions of all processes are uniquely defined in round $k + 1$ due to the fact that the exchanged messages of round $k + 1$ are completely determined by actions taken until round k.

7.3 FEASIBILITY OF *AD HOC* BROADCAST

The Certified Propagation Algorithm (CPA, pseudo-code in Algorithm 7.15), proposed in [45], uses only local information and thus is particularly suitable for *ad hoc* networks. CPA is probably the only safe broadcast algorithm known up to now for the f-locally bounded model, which does not require knowledge of the network topology or uses topology discovery subroutines. CPA assumes that each process knows the id of its neighbors (as is assumed for any algorithm any *ad hoc* algorithm) and the id of the sender s. Observe that, unlike the previously presented consensus algorithms, a process in CPA executes a different part of the code depending on its id.

Algorithm 7.15 CPA (Certified-Propagation-Algorithm)

(For process $i \in V$)

1: **if** $i = s$ **then** $\qquad\qquad\qquad\qquad\qquad\qquad\qquad\qquad$ ▷ *Code for s*
2: $\quad$ Send value $x_s \in X$ to all neighbors, decide on x_s and terminate.
3: **else if** $i \in N_s$ **then** $\qquad\qquad\qquad\qquad\qquad\qquad$ ▷ *Code for neighbors of s*
4: $\quad$ Upon reception of x_s from the sender, decide on x_s, send it to all neighbors and terminate.
5: **else if** $i \notin N_s \cup s$ **then** $\qquad\qquad\qquad\qquad\qquad$ ▷ *Code for all other nodes*
6: $\quad$ Upon reception of $f + 1$ messages with the same value x from $f + 1$ distinct neighbors, decide on x, send it to all neighbors and terminate.
7: **end if**

As shown in [45], CPA is an f-locally safe broadcast algorithm. The proof is presented below.

Theorem 7.9 *CPA is f-locally safe.*

Proof. We will show that if a process decides on a value x through CPA then $x = x_s$. Assume, on the contrary, that there is a set of processes $V' \subseteq V$ that decide on values different than x_s. Let i be the process of V' that decides in the earliest round among all processes in V', i.e., the first process to make an incorrect decision, and assume that i decides on $x \neq x_s$. Process i cannot be a neighbor of the sender since all neighbors of the sender only decide on x_s as can be shown in the respective decision rule of CPA. Therefore, i has received $f + 1$ copies of x from $f + 1$ distinct neighbors. Since at most $t(v)$ neighbors can be corrupted, at least one fault-free process has decided in $x \neq x_s$ before i. A contradiction to the fact that i is the first process to make an incorrect decision. $\qquad\qquad\square$

Condition PLC proves to be sufficient for CPA to achieve broadcast, as can be seen in the following.

Theorem 7.10 Sufficient Condition. *If (G, s) satisfies condition PLC, then CPA is f-locally resilient for (G, s).*

Proof. Suppose that PLC holds and thus, no f-plp cut exists in G. Assume an execution of CPA where the actual corruption set is F. By definition, F is f-local, since we are in the f-locally bounded adversary model; clearly $F \cup N_s$ is a cut on G as defined before (i.e., not including process s). Since F is f-local and $F \cup N_s$ is not a f-plp cut there must exist $i_1 \in V \setminus (F \cup N_s \cup s)$ s.t. $|Ni_1 \cap (N_s \setminus F)| \geq f + 1$. Since i_1 is fault-free and all processes in $N_s \setminus F$ will trivially decide on the correct value x_s through CPA as direct neighbors of the sender, i_1 will receive f copies of x_s and decide on the *correct* sender's value x_s. Let us now use the same argument inductively to show that every fault-free process will eventually decide on the *correct* value x_s through CPA. Let $C_k = (N_s \setminus F) \cup \{i_1, i_2, ..., i_{k-1}\}$ be the set of the fault-free processes that have decided until a certain round of the protocol, and assume that they decided on the correct value x_s. Then $C_k \cup F$ is a cut. Since F is f-local, by the same argument as before there exists a process i_k s.t. $|C_k \cap N_{i_k}| \geq f + 1$ and i_k will decide *correctly* on x_s. Eventually all fault-free processes will *correctly* decide on x_s. Thus, CPA is f-locally resilient in G. $\square$

The following corollary is immediate from Theorems 7.10 and 7.8.

Corollary 7.11   CPA Optimality   *Given a graph G and sender s, if there exists an ad hoc broadcast algorithm which is f-locally resilient in (G, s) and f-locally safe, then CPA is f-locally resilient in (G, s).*

The f-local Safety Requirement   We can show that if we drop the requirement for f-local safety, then Theorem 7.8 does not hold. Intuitively, the reason is that an *ad hoc* protocol that assumes certain topological properties for the network may be f-locally resilient in a family of graphs that have the assumed topological properties. Indeed, Pelc and Peleg [79] introduced the *Relaxed Propagation Algorithm* (RPA) which uses knowledge of the topology of the network and they proved that there exists a graph G'' with sender s for which RPA is 1-locally resilient and CPA is not. So if we use RPA in an *ad hoc* setting assuming that the network is G'' then this algorithm will be f-locally resilient for (G'', s) while CPA will not. Non-f-local safety of RPA follows from the fact that the decisions depend on the assumed topology and therefore they could be incorrect if the topological assumptions do not hold. More specifically, a process, running RPA, could decide on a message which it receives from $2f + 1$ disjoint paths and for which it can verify, from the assumed topology, that at most f may contain corrupted processes. However, if the topology is actually not as assumed, then it could even be the case that all $2f + 1$ paths contain corrupted processes and thus the decision value is incorrect. The fact that the non-safe algorithm RPA is resilient in instances where CPA is not shows that there exist non-safe algorithms of higher local resilience than CPA.

7.4   RELATION WITH CONSENSUS FEASIBILITY

It is well known by results in [50] that Byzantine exact consensus in complete graphs is feasible if and only if $n > 3t$, where t is the overall number of corruptions in the network. Given a graph

G and local corruption bound f let t be the maximum overall number of corruptions that can be performed by the local adversary, i.e.,

$$t = \max_{\substack{F : f\text{-local set} \\ F \subseteq V}} |F|.$$

The next corollary yields from the feasibility condition $n > 3t$, from the tightness of the non-existence of an f-plp cut for the feasibility of broadcast and the fact that, given a broadcast subprotocol, one can simulate any consensus solution for complete graphs. The proof is similar to that of Theorem 2.3.

Corollary 7.12   *For a graph $G = (V, E)$, $|V| = n$ and $f, F \in \mathbb{N}$, if $n > 3t$ and there does not exist an f-plp cut for any sender-process $s \in V$, then exact consensus in G under an f-local adversary is feasible.*

Observe that the condition is *not* necessary due to the fact that we consider only safe algorithms for broadcast.

7.5   MODEL EXTENSIONS

7.5.1   NON-UNIFORM MODEL

The results presented up to now for the f-local adversary model have been proven in [73], that trivially extend to the *non-uniform f-local adversary model*; this model allows for a varying bound on the number of corruptions in each process' neighborhood and is concretely described below.

Non-Uniform f-Local Adversary Model.   Given graph $G = (V, E)$ and sender s, let the *corruption function $f : V \to \mathbb{N}$*. A non-uniform f-local adversary can corrupt at most $f(u)$ processes in the neighborhood N_u of each process $u \in V$.

The results already presented for the local adversary case can be trivially extended to the non-uniform case by using the following definition for the notion of a f-local set.

Definition 7.13   (non-uniform) f-local set.   Given a graph $G = (V, E)$ and a function $t : V \to \mathbb{N}$ a *f-local set* is a set $C \subseteq V$ for which $\forall u \in V$, $|N_u \cap C| \leq t(u)$. For $V' \subseteq V$ a *f-local w.r.t. V' set* is a set $C \subseteq V$ for which $\forall u \in V'$, $|N_u \cap C| \leq t(u)$.

7.5.2   DIRECTED NETWORKS

Considering directed graphs, the general definition of the local adversary model presented in Section 1.2.1 states that the adversary can corrupt at most f incoming neighbors of each process. Naturally, The definition of the f-plp cut can be easily extended to the directed network case by simply replacing the notion of a neighborhood N_v with the notion of the incoming neighborhood N_v^- in Definition 7.2 of a f-local set. In the following, we will use the latter definition of the f-local set.

An equivalent condition to that of the non-existence of the f-plp cut, especially tailored for the directed network case, was proposed by Tseng, Vaidya, and Bhandari in [89]. In particular, the authors define the following notion of redundant propagation which allows for the extraction of the necessary and sufficient condition presented below.

Definition 7.14   Given non-empty disjoint sets of processes A and B, we will say that $A \rightarrow B$ iff there exists a process $v \in B$ that has at least $f + 1$ distinct incoming neighbors in A, i.e., $|N^-(v) \cap A| > f$. The negation of $A \rightarrow B$ will be denoted with $A \nrightarrow B$

The following condition is proved in [89] to be necessary and sufficient for the correctness of CPA.

Theorem 7.15   *CPA achieves broadcast in (G, s) if and only if, for any partition F, L, R of V, where (i) the sender $s \in L$, (ii) R is non-empty, and (iii) F is a f-local set, at least one of the following holds.*

- $L \rightarrow R$

- *R contains an outgoing neighbor of s, i.e., $N_s^+ \cap R \neq \emptyset$*

The condition can be easily proven equivalent with the condition of Corollary 7.11 in its directed case variation. Therefore, the above condition also is tight for the existence of a correct t-locally safe *ad hoc* broadcast algorithm in directed networks.

7.6   MAXIMUM TOLERABLE NUMBER OF LOCAL FAULTS

Checking condition PLC by evaluating the existence of a f-plp cut in a given network is an issue of practical importance. It is crucial for a system designer to determine if broadcast can be reliably performed in the given network for a given f or even estimate the maximum f that can be locally tolerated. In [73], it is shown that deciding if a f-plp cut exists is an NP-hard problem; moreover, it is also observed that the latter negative result has a positive aspect, namely, that a polynomially bounded adversary is unable to design an optimal attack unless P = NP.

On the other hand, in [41, 56], the authors addressed the issue of approximating the maximum number of corrupted processes $f_{\max}^{\text{CPA}}$ that CPA can tolerate under the f-locally bounded adversary model. By Corollary 7.11, it is clear that $f_{\max}^{\text{CPA}}$ denotes also the maximum number of local corruptions that any safe *ad hoc* broadcast algorithm can tolerate. In the following, we will present the approximation result, adopting notions from [56]. These notions were recently generalized in [15] in order to address the same problem in dynamic networks.

Definition 7.16   Max CPA Resilience.   For a graph G and sender s, $f_{\max}^{\text{CPA}}(G, s)$ is the maximum f such that CPA is f-locally resilient.

Whenever G and s are implied by the context, we will simply write $f_{\max}^{CPA}$. The following notions are proven useful for the determination of lower and upper bounds on $f_{\max}^{CPA}$. Intuitively, a minimum k-level ordering is an arrangement of processes-nodes into disjoint levels, such that every process has at least k neighbors in previous levels and belongs to the minimum level for which this property is satisfied for this process. Formally, we have the following.

Definition 7.17   Minimum k-Level Ordering.   A *minimum k-level ordering* $\mathcal{L}_k(G, s)$ of a graph $G = (V, E)$ for a given sender s is a partition $V \setminus \{s\} = \bigcup_{h=1}^{m} L_h$, $m \in \mathbb{N}$ such that

$$L_1 = N_s,$$

$$L_h = \{i \in V \setminus \bigcup_{t=1}^{h-1} L_j : |N_i \cap \bigcup_{t=1}^{h-1} L_t| \geq k\}, 2 \leq h \leq m.$$

The next definition of the relaxed k-level ordering notion will be useful for the presented proofs and is acquired by dropping the level minimality requirement for processes-nodes.

Definition 7.18   Relaxed k-Level Ordering.   A *relaxed k-level ordering* of a graph $G = (V, E)$ for a given sender s is a partition $V \setminus \{s\} = \bigcup_{h=1}^{m} L_h$, $m \in \mathbb{N}$ s.t.

$$L_1 = N_s, \qquad \forall i \in L_h : |N_i \cap \bigcup_{t=1}^{h-1} L_t| \geq k.$$

Note that while there may exist several relaxed k-level orderings of a graph, the minimum k-level ordering is unique, as can be shown by an easy induction. Also, as pointed out in [56], a relaxed k-level ordering may be easily transformed to the unique minimum k-level ordering.

Definition 7.19   Parameter $\mathcal{K}$.   For pair (G, s) we define,

$$\mathcal{K}(G, s) = \max\{k \in \mathbb{N} \mid \exists \text{ a minimum } k\text{-level ordering } \mathcal{L}_k(G, s)\}$$

7.6.1   BOUNDS ON MAX CPA RESILIENCE

The following theorems state sufficient and necessary conditions for the correctness of CPA which, in turn, naturally imply upper and lower bounds on $f_{\max}^{CPA}$.

Theorem 7.20   Sufficient Condition.   *For every graph G, sender s and $f \in \mathbb{N}$, if $f < \mathcal{K}(G, s)/2$ then CPA is f-locally resilient.*

Proof. Observe that $2f < \mathcal{K}(G, s)$ implies the existence of a minimum $(2f + 1)$-level ordering $\mathcal{L}_{2f+1}(G, s)$. Let $\mathcal{L}_{2f+1}(G, s)$ be the partition $\{L_1, \ldots, L_m\}$ of V, i.e., $V = \bigcup_{h=1}^{m} L_i$. It suffices to show that for $1 \le h \le m$, every fault-free process $i \in L_h$ decides on the sender's value x_s. By strong induction on h, every fault-free process $i \in L_1 = N_s$ decides on the sender's value x_s due to the CPA steps 1 and 2. If all fault-free processes $j \in L_h, 1 \le h \le l$, decide on x_s at some round, then every fault-free process $i \in L_{l+1}$ receives $|\bigcup_{h=1}^{l} L_h \cap N_i| \ge 2f + 1$ messages from its decided neighbors in previous levels and at least $f + 1$ of them are fault-free. Thus, i decides on x_s. $\square$

Theorem 7.21 Necessary Condition. *For any graph G, sender s and $f \ge \mathcal{K}(G, s)$, CPA is not f-locally resilient.*

Proof. Assume that CPA is f-locally resilient, with $f \ge \mathcal{K}(G, s)$. Since, by assumption, CPA is f-locally resilient there must be a positive integer, let T, so that the algorithm terminates after T steps in G. Consider now the operation of CPA on graph G in terms of sets. Let L_h denote the set of processes that decide in the h-th round. Since every process in L_h decides at the h-th round we get that it has at least $f + 1$ neighbors in sets $L_1, \ldots, L_{h-1}$. That is,

$$\forall i \in L_h \Rightarrow |N_i \cap \bigcup_{t=1}^{h-1} L_t| \ge f + 1.$$ Observe that the above sequence is a relaxed $(f + 1)$-level ordering for G, s, and it can be defined up to $h = T$. From the above observation and the fact that the existence of a relaxed level ordering implies the existence of a minimum one, we get that there must be a minimum $(f + 1)$-level ordering for G, s. But this is a contradiction since we assumed that $f \ge \mathcal{K}(G, s)$. $\square$

The following Corollary follows immediately from Theorems 7.20 and 7.21.

Corollary 7.22 Bounds on $f_{\max}^{\text{CPA}}$ *For any graph G and sender s, it holds that*

$$\lceil \mathcal{K}(G, s)/2 \rceil - 1 \le f_{\max}^{\text{CPA}} < \mathcal{K}(G, s).$$

7.6.2 EFFICIENT APPROXIMATION OF MAX CPA RESILIENCE

In the following, we present an efficient 2-approximation algorithm for *Max CPA Resilience*, proposed in [56]. The existence of a minimum m-level ordering for (G, s) can be checked by Algorithm 7.16, a slight variation of the standard BFS algorithm. Subsequently, the approximation can be obtained by using the above check in the context of a binary search (Algorithm 7.17). The ratio follows immediately, by Corollary 7.22. Note that Algorithm 7.16 can be used to compute the minimum m-level ordering $\mathcal{L}_m(G, s)$.

Algorithm 7.16 Existence check of a minimum m-level ordering for (G, s)

Initialization: Assign a zero counter to each process.

1: Enqueue the sender and every one of its neighbors.
2: Dequeue a process and increase the counters of all its neighbors. Enqueue a neighbor only if its counter is at least m.
3: Repeat Step 3 until the queue is empty.
4: If all processes have been enqueued then output '*True*' (a minimum m-level ordering exists); otherwise, output '*False*'.

Algorithm 7.17 2-Approximation of $f_{\max}^{\mathrm{CPA}}$

1: Compute $\mathcal{K}(G, s)$: since $\mathcal{K}(G, s) < \min_{v \in V \setminus (N_s \cup s)} \deg(v) = \delta$, the exact value of $\mathcal{K}(G, s)$ is computed by $\log \delta$ repetitions of the existence check, by simple binary search.
2: Return $\lceil \mathcal{K}(G, s)/2 \rceil - 1$.

Since $t \geq \mathcal{K}(G, s)$ implies that CPA is not f-locally resilient, it holds that $f_{\max}^{\mathrm{CPA}} < \mathcal{K}(G, s)$; consequently, the returned value is at least $\lceil f_{\max}^{\mathrm{CPA}}/2 \rceil - 1$. A tight example for the approximation ratio of the algorithm is given by the instance in Figure 7.2 for which $\mathcal{K}(G, s) = f + 1$ and CPA is f-locally resilient, as proved in [56]. In this instance the neighborhood of s consists of $2t^2 + 2f$ processes which form a clique of size $2f$ and are connected with N_s as shown in the figure.

The complexity of the above approximation algorithm is obviously given by the complexity of the computation of $\mathcal{K}(G, s)$. As explained above, the algorithm requires at most $\log \delta$ executions of the existence check. The latter requires $O(|E|)$ time (same complexity as BFS). Altogether, we get that the time complexity of the algorithm is $O(|E| \log \delta)$.

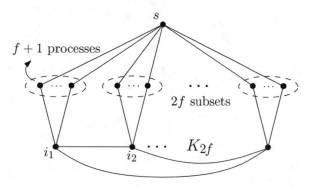

Figure 7.2: A tight example for the approximation ratio.

CHAPTER 8

General Adversary

In the final chapter, we deal with the feasibility of consensus and related problems under restricted knowledge assumptions and the *general adversary model*, originally proposed by Hirt and Maurer in [40]. This model encompasses all known adversary models with respect to the definition of corruptible sets. Specifically, the corruptible sets of processes are described by a monotone family of sets.

Section 8.1 considers the feasibility of approximate consensus through IAC algorithms under a general Byzantine adversary; the presented results first appeared in the work of Tseng and Vaidya [94] and assume that topology knowledge of processes is restricted to their immediate neighborhood. Section 8.2 refers to the *reliable message transmission* problem (RMT) under a general adversary. The problem is considered in the *partial knowledge model* [73] where each process may know a specific subgraph of the network. Observe that if RMT is achieved between all pairs of processes in the network, then consensus can be achieved by simulating a complete network and executing any protocol for complete networks; this argument is formalized in Corollary 8.17 in the end of the chapter and is similar to the argument presented in the context of broadcast in Corollary 7.12. Therefore, the presented condition also yields a sufficient condition for exact consensus as can be shown by a variation of Theorem 2.3. The results of Section 8.2 were first presented in [74] by Pagourtzis, Panagiotakos and Sakavalas.

The General Byzantine Adversary Model   In the rest of the chapter, we assume a Byzantine adversary which can make processes deviate arbitrarily from the executed protocol. Regarding the corruptible sets, we will use the *general adversary* model, defined in Section 1.2.1. We remind that in this model, given a monotone family $\mathcal{F}$ of subsets of V, called the adversary structure (or fault domain), a set F is corruptible (or a *feasible* fault set) if and only if $F \in \mathcal{F}$.

Thus, each set in $\mathcal{F}$ specifies processes that may all potentially fail during a single execution of the algorithm. This feature can be used to capture the notion of correlated failures. For example, consider a system consisting of four processes, namely, processes 1, 2, 3, and 4. Suppose that

$$\mathcal{F} = \{\{1\}, \{2\}, \{3, 4\}\}.$$

This definition of $\mathcal{F}$ implies that during an execution either (i) process 1 may fail, (ii) process 2 may fail, or (iii) any subset of $\{3, 4\}$ may fail, and no other combination of processes may fail (e.g., processes 1 and 3 cannot both fail in a single execution). In this case, the reason that the set $\{3, 4\}$ is in the fault domain may be that the failures of processes 3 and 4 are correlated.

The generalized fault model is also useful to capture variations in process reliability [40, 43, 47]. For instance, in the above example, processes 1 and 2 may be more reliable than processes 3 and 4. Therefore, while processes 3 and 4 may fail in the same execution, processes 1 and 2 are less likely to fail together in the same execution. Therefore, $\{1, 2\} \notin \mathcal{F}$.

8.1 APPROXIMATE BYZANTINE CONSENSUS UNDER A GENERAL ADVERSARY

Here, we present the results of [94] on the feasibility of approximate Byzantine consensus in arbitrary directed networks against a general adversary. Specifically, we present the necessary and sufficient condition on the underlying communication graph for the existence of IAC algorithms for this setting.

8.1.1 IMPOSSIBILITY OF APPROXIMATE CONSENSUS

To determine the topological necessary and sufficient condition for approximate consensus to be feasible in this setting we will use the notions of *source component* and *reduced graph* previously presented in Definitions 5.5 and 5.6, respectively. Next we define the Condition SCR (Source-Component-Reduced).

Definition 8.1 Condition SCR. Any reduced graph G_F corresponding to any feasible fault set F contains exactly one *source component*.

The impossibility result follows.

Theorem 8.2 *Suppose that a correct synchronous IAC algorithm exists for $G = (V, E)$. Then, G satisfies Condition SCR.*

Proof Sketch: A complete proof is presented in [87]. The proof is by contradiction. Let us assume that a correct IAC algorithm exists, and for some feasible fault set F, and feasible sets $F_x(i)$ for each $i \in V \setminus F$, the resulting reduced graph contains two source components. Let L and R denote the processes in the two source components, respectively. Thus, L and R are disjoint and non-empty. Let $C = V \setminus (F \cup L \cup R)$ be the remaining processes in the reduced graph. Set C may or may not be non-empty. Assume that the processes in F (if non-empty) are all faulty, and all the processes in L, R, and C (if non-empty) are fault-free. Suppose that each process in L has initial input equal to m, each process in R has initial input equal to M, where $M > m$, and each process in C has an input in the range $[m, M]$. As elaborated in [87], the faulty processes can behave in such a manner that, in each iteration, processes in L and R are forced to maintain their updated state equal to m and M, respectively, so as to satisfy the validity condition. This ensures that, no matter how many iterations are performed, the convergence condition cannot be satisfied. □

8.1.2   GENERAL ADVERSARY IAC ALGORITHM

We next present Algorithm 8.18 G-IAC (General adversary IAC), a synchronous IAC algorithm proposed in [94], which satisfies the validity and convergence conditions provided that the graph $G = (V, E)$ satisfies the necessary Condition SCR. Since Condition SCR is shown to be necessary (Theorem 8.2). This implies that the Condition SCR in is also sufficient.

Local Knowledge of $\mathcal{F}$ It may first appear that it is expensive to specify the generalized fault model, since the size might be exponential to the size of the network. Fortunately, to implement Algorithm G-IAC, it is sufficient for each process i to know $N_i^- \cap F$, for each feasible fault set F. In other words, each process only needs to know the set of its incoming neighbors that may fail in the same execution of the algorithm. Thus, the iterative algorithm can be implemented using only "local" information regarding $\mathcal{F}$.

Comparison   Algorithm G-IAC is a generalization—to accommodate the generalized fault model—of iterative algorithms that were analyzed in prior work [28, 54, 58, 98]. The key difference from previous algorithms is in the *Update* step of Algorithm G-IAC. The steps need to be followed by all the fault-free processes in round t ($t > 0$) are described in Algorithm 8.18.

The main difference between the Algorithm G-IAC and other IAC algorithms presented lies in the choice of the values eliminated from vector $r_i[t]$ in the *Update* step. The manner in which the values are eliminated ensures that the values received from processes $D(f_1 + 1)$ and $D(|N_i^-| - f_2 + 1)$ (i.e., the smallest and largest values that survive in $r_i[t]$) are within the convex hull of the state of fault-free processes, even if processes $D(f_1 + 1)$ and $D(|N_i^-| - f_2 + 1)$ may not be fault-free. This property is useful in proving algorithm correctness (as discussed below).

Observe that $f_1 + f_2$ processes whose values are eliminated in the *Update* step above are all in N_i^-. Thus, the above algorithm can be implemented by process i if it knows which of its incoming neighbors may fail in a single execution of the algorithm; process i does not need to know the entire fault domain $\mathcal{F}$ as such.

Correctness of Algorithm G-IAC   In [94], it is proved that Algorithm G-IAC satisfies the validity and convergence conditions, provided that $G = (V, E)$ satisfies Condition SCR (Definition 8.1) which is also necessary by Theorem 8.2. Observe that as the algorithm is stated, no termination occurs; thus, the proof of [94] argue that there exists some round in which the state values of all fault-free processes will be in distance ϵ from each other. However, the termination property can be shown to hold in the same way it holds for analogous algorithms presented in [28, 44, 58].

While we believe that the correctness of Algorithm G-IAC can be proved similarly using the approach presented in earlier chapters. In [94], Tseng and Vaidya presented a novel matrix-based proof which model the state evolution of each fault-free process. A similar proof was later used to prove the correctness of other iterative consensus algorithms [91, 92].

Algorithm 8.18 G-IAC (General-adversary-IAC)

(For process $i \in V$)
Initialization: $v_i[0] :=$ input of node i

1: *Transmit step:* Transmit current state $v_i[t-1]$ on all outgoing edges and self-loop.
2: *Receive step:* Receive values on all incoming edges and self-loop. These values form vector $r_i[t]$ of size $|N_i^-| + 1$ (including the value from process i itself). When a fault-free process expects to receive a message from an incoming neighbor but does not receive the message, the message value is assumed to be equal to its own state, i.e., $v_i[t-1]$.
3: *Update step:* Sort the values in $r_i[t]$ in an increasing order (breaking ties arbitrarily). Let D be a vector of processes arranged in an order "consistent" with $r_i[t]$: specifically, $D(1)$ is the process that sent the smallest value in $r_i[t]$, $D(2)$ is the process that sent the second smallest value in $r_i[t]$, and so on. The size of vector D is also $|N_i^-| + 1$.
From vector $r_i[t]$, eliminate the smallest f_1 values, and the largest f_2 values, where f_1 and f_2 are defined as follows.

- f_1 is the largest number such that there exists a feasible fault set $F' \subseteq N_i^-$ containing processes $D(1), D(2), ..., D(f_1)$. Recall that $i \notin N_i^-$.

- f_2 is the largest number such that there exists a feasible fault set $F'' \subseteq N_i^-$ containing processes $D(|N_i^-| - f_2 + 2), D(|N_i^-| - f_2 + 3), ..., D(|N_i^-| + 1)$.

F' and F'' above may or may not be identical.
Let $N_i^*[t]$ denote the set of processes from whom the remaining $|N_i^-| + 1 - f_1 - f_2$ values in $r_i[t]$ were received, and let w_j denote the value received from process $j \in N_i^*[t]$. Note that $i \in N_i^*[t]$. Hence, for convenience, define $w_i = v_i[t-1]$ to be the value process i receives from itself. Observe that if $j \in N_i^*[t]$ is fault-free, then $w_j = v_j[t-1]$. Define:

$$v_i[t] \;=\; Z_i(r_i[t]) \;=\; \sum_{j \in N_i^*[t]} a_i\, w_j, \text{ where } a_i = \frac{1}{|N_i^*[t]|} = \frac{1}{|N_i^-| + 1 - f_1 - f_2}.$$

The "weight" of each term on the right-hand side of (5.1) is a_i, and these weights add to 1. Also, $0 < a_i \leq 1$. Although f_1, f_2, and a_i may be different for each iteration t, for simplicity, we do not explicitly represent this dependence on t in the notations.

8.2   RELIABLE COMMUNICATION UNDER PARTIAL TOPOLOGY KNOWLEDGE

In this section, we consider the fundamental primitive of *Reliable Message Transmission* (RMT), which refers to the task of correctly sending a message from a process to another, despite the presence of Byzantine corruptions. We assume an *undirected network* and present the results of [74], where the initial knowledge possessed by the processes is explicitly considered. For that, the recently introduced *Partial Knowledge Model* [73] and the general adversary model [40] are employed. In the partial knowledge model, a process has knowledge over an arbitrary subgraph of the network. A tight condition for the feasibility of RMT in the setting resulting from the combination of these two quite general models is presented. The presented condition also yields a sufficient condition for exact consensus. This can be shown by a variation of Theorem 2.3 which considers RMT to simulate any consensus protocol for complete networks in the case of an incomplete network.

The motivation for partial knowledge considerations comes from large-scale networks (e.g., the Internet or sensor networks) where topologically local estimation of the power of the adversary may be possible, while global estimation may be hard to obtain due to geographical or jurisdiction constraints. Additionally, proximity in social networks is often correlated with an increased amount of available information, further justifying the relevance of the model.

8.2.1   PRELIMINARIES

The formal definition of the problem has been given in Definition 2.1. In the following, we present the *partial knowledge mode*, originally introduced in [73]. For ease of presentation, we will adopt the notation $G = (V, E)$ for the graph consisting of the process (node) set $V(G)$ and edge set $E(G)$.

The Partial Knowledge Model   In this setting, each process i only has knowledge of the topology of a certain subgraph G_i of G which includes i. Namely, if we consider the family $\mathcal{G}$ of subgraphs of G we use the *view function* $\gamma : V(G) \to \mathcal{G}$, where $\gamma(i)$ represents the subgraph of G over which process i has knowledge of the topology. We extend the domain of γ by allowing as input a set $S \subseteq V(G)$. The output will correspond to the *joint view* of processes in S. More specifically, if $\gamma(i) = G_i = (V_i, E_i)$, then $\gamma(S) = G_S = (\bigcup_{i \in S} V_i, \bigcup_{i \in S} E_i)$. The extensively studied *ad hoc* model (cf. [79]) as well as the model considered in Section 8.1 can be seen as special cases of the Partial Knowledge Model, where the topology knowledge of each process is limited to its own neighborhood, i.e., $\forall i \in V(G), \ \gamma(i) = N(i)$.

In order to capture partial knowledge in the general adversary model, we need to define the restriction of some structure to a set of processes.

Definition 8.3   Adversary Structure $\mathcal{E}$.   For an adversary structure $\mathcal{E}$ and a process set A, let $\mathcal{E}^A = \{F \cap A \mid F \in \mathcal{E}\}$ denote the restriction of $\mathcal{E}$ to the set A.

Local Adversary Structure In the following, we assume that given the actual adversary structure $\mathcal{F}$, each process i only knows the possible corruption sets under its view $\mathcal{F}_i$, which is equal to $\mathcal{F}^{V(\gamma(i))}$ (the *local adversary structure*). Observe that this is a generalization of the knowledge model considered in Section 8.1. We denote an instance of the problem by the tuple $\mathcal{I} = (G, \mathcal{F}, \gamma, s, r)$. We next define some useful protocol properties.

Analogously with the term "fault tolerant" used previously in the book, we will now say that an algorithm is *resilient* for instance $\mathcal{I}$. More concretely, we have the following.

Definition 8.4 Resilient Algorithm for Instance I. An algorithm which achieves RMT in an instance $\mathcal{I} = (G, \mathcal{F}, \gamma, s, r)$ for any corruption set $F \in \mathcal{F}$ and any behavior of F is called *resilient* for $\mathcal{I}$.

We say that an RMT protocol is *safe* if it never causes the receiver r to decide on an incorrect value in any instance. The importance of the safety property is pointed out in [79], where it is regarded as a basic requirement of a Broadcast algorithm; similarly, in the case of RMT, it guarantees that if the receiver does not have sufficient information to decide on the sender's value, she won't eventually decide on an incorrect value or accept false data. The formal definition is as follows.

Definition 8.5 Safe Algorithm. An algorithm which never causes a fault-free process to decide on (output) an incorrect value, for any instance $I = (G, \mathcal{F}, \gamma, s, r)$ and any adversarial behavior, is called *safe*.

8.2.2 THE ALGEBRAIC STRUCTURE OF PARTIAL KNOWLEDGE

In this section, we consider the algebraic structure of the knowledge of processes regarding the adversary. This has been analyzed in [74], by defining an operation to calculate their joint knowledge. As is shown in the same work, this operation allows the combination of local knowledge in an optimal way. The operation takes into account potentially different adversarial structures, so that it is well defined even if a corrupted process provides a different structure than the real one to some fault-free process.

Definition 8.6 Let V be a finite node set; let also $\mathbb{T} = \{(\mathcal{E}, A) \mid \mathcal{E} \subseteq 2^A, A \subseteq V, \ \mathcal{E} \text{ is monotone}\}$ denote the space of all pairs consisting of a monotone family of subsets of a node set along with that node set. The operation $\oplus : \mathbb{T} \times \mathbb{T} \to \mathbb{T}$ is defined as follows:

$$(\mathcal{E}, A) \oplus (\mathcal{D}, B) = (\{F_1 \cup F_2 \mid (F_1 \in \mathcal{E}) \wedge (F_2 \in \mathcal{D}) \wedge (F_1 \cap B = F_2 \cap A)\}, A \cup B).$$

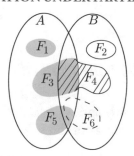

Figure 8.1: Example of the joint knowledge operation $\oplus$.

Informally, $(\mathcal{E}, A) \oplus (\mathcal{D}, B)$ unites possible corruption sets from $\mathcal{E}$ and $\mathcal{D}$ that "agree" on $A \cap B$. For instance, in Figure 8.1 we present an example of the operation between pairs $(\mathcal{E}, A), (\mathcal{D}, B)$ with $\mathcal{E} = \{F_1, F_3, F_5\}$, $\mathcal{D} = \{F_2, F_4, F_6\}$; for $(\mathcal{E}, A) \oplus (\mathcal{D}, B) = (\mathcal{H}, A \cup B)$, we observe that $F_1 \cup F_2$ and $F_3 \cup F_4$ belong to $\mathcal{H}$ while $F_5 \cup F_6$ and $F_1 \cup F_4$ do not.

The following theorem offers further insight on the algebraic properties of this operation, by revealing a semilattice structure on the space of partial knowledge obtained by the processes. The semilattice structure is shown by proving the commutativity, associativity and idempotence properties of operation $\oplus$. The proof of the following theorem can be found in [74].

Theorem 8.7 $\langle \mathbb{T}, \oplus \rangle$ *is a semilattice.*

The semilattice properties imply the following theorem, which states a property of the $\oplus$ operation which is important in the study of RMT. The proof is presented in [74].

Theorem 8.8   *For any adversary structure $\mathcal{F}$ and process sets A, B:*

$$\text{if } (\mathcal{H}, A \cup B) = (\mathcal{F}^A, A) \oplus (\mathcal{F}^B, B) \text{ then } \mathcal{F}^{(A \cup B)} \subseteq \mathcal{H}.$$

Theorem 8.8 implies that the $\oplus$ operation gives the maximal (w.r.t inclusion) possible adversary structure that is indistinguishable by two processes that know $\mathcal{F}^A$ and $\mathcal{F}^B$, respectively, i.e., it coincides with their knowledge of the adversary structures on sets A and B, respectively.

Now recall that $\mathcal{F}_i = \mathcal{F}^{V(\gamma(i))}$. This allows us to define the combined knowledge of a set of processes B about the adversary structure $\mathcal{F}$ as follows. For a given adversary structure $\mathcal{F}$, a view function γ, and a process set B, let

$$(\mathcal{F}_B, V(\gamma(B))) = \bigoplus_{i \in B}(\mathcal{F}_i, V(\gamma(i))) = \bigoplus_{i \in B}(\mathcal{F}^{V(\gamma(i))}, V(\gamma(i))).$$

Note that $\mathcal{F}_B$ exactly captures the maximal adversary structure possible, restricted in $\gamma(B)$, relative to the initial knowledge of processes in B. Also notice that using Theorem 8.8 we get $\mathcal{F}^{V(\gamma(B))} \subseteq \mathcal{F}_B$. The interpretation of this inclusion in our setting is that what processes in B

conceive as the worst case adversary structure indistinguishable to them *always* contains the actual adversary structure in their scenario.

8.2.3   NECESSARY TOPOLOGICAL CONDITION

We assume that the sender knows the id of process r. As mentioned, an instance of the problem by the tuple $(G, \mathcal{F}, \gamma, s, r)$. The following notion of an RMT-cut has been proven instrumental to the analysis of RMT feasibility by safe algorithms.

Definition 8.9   RMT-cut.   Let $(G, \mathcal{T}, \gamma, s, r)$ be an RMT instance and $C = C_1 \cup C_2$ be a cut in G, partitioning $V \setminus C$ in two sets $A, B' \neq \emptyset$ where $s \in A$ and $r \in B'$. Let $B \subseteq B'$ be the node set of the connected component that r lies in. Then C is a *RMT-cut* iff $C_1 \in \mathcal{F}$ and $C_2 \cap V(\gamma(B)) \in \mathcal{F}_B$.

For ease of presentation, we define Condition GRC (General-Reliablity-Cut) as follows.

Definition 8.10   Condition GRC.   We will say that Condition GRC holds in an RMT instance whenever there *does not* exist an RMT-cut in that instance.

The necessary condition proof adapts techniques and ideas from [73, 79] to model of partial knowledge model under a general adversary and has been presented originally in [74].

Theorem 8.11   Necessity.   *A safe and resilient RMT algorithm exists only for instances where Condition GRC holds.*

Proof.   Assume Condition GRC does not hold in instance $(G, \mathcal{F}, \gamma, s, r)$. Let $C = C_1 \cup C_2$ be the RMT-cut which partitions $V \setminus C$ in sets $A, B \neq \emptyset$ s.t. $s \in A$ and $r \in B$. Without loss of generality assume that B is connected. If it is not, then by adding to A all nodes that do not belong to the connected component of r, an RMT-cut with the desired property is obtained. Consider a second instance where $\mathcal{F}' = \mathcal{F}_B$ and all other parameters are the same as in the original instance. Recall that $\mathcal{F}_B$ is defined using the $\oplus$ operator and exactly captures (by Corollary 8.8) the worst case adversary structure possible, restricted to $V(\gamma(B))$, relative to the initial knowledge of processes in B. Hence, all processes in B have the same initial knowledge in both instances, since $\mathcal{F}_B = \mathcal{F}'_B$.

The proof is by contradiction. Suppose that there exists a safe algorithm $\mathcal{A}$ which is resilient for $(G, \mathcal{F}, \gamma, s, r)$. We consider the following executions σ and σ' of $\mathcal{A}$.

- Execution σ is on instance $(G, \mathcal{F}, \gamma, s, r)$, with sender's value $x_s = 0$, and corruption set C_1; in each round, each corrupted process in C_1 performs the actions that its corresponding process performs in the respective round of execution σ' (where C_1 consists of fault-free processes only).

- Execution σ' is on instance $(G, \mathcal{F}', \gamma, s, r)$, with sender's value $x_s = 1$, and corruption set C_2; in each round, each corrupted process in C_2 performs the actions that its corresponding process performs in the respective round of execution σ (where C_2 consists of fault-free processes only).

Note that C_1, C_2 are admissible corruption sets in scenarios σ, σ', respectively, since they belong to $\mathcal{F}$ and $\mathcal{F}'$ (resp.). It is easy to see that $C_1 \cup C_2$ is a cut which separates s from B in both instances and that actions of every process of this cut are identical in both executions σ, σ'. Consequently, the actions of any fault-free process $i \in B$ must be identical in both executions. Since, by assumption, algorithm $\mathcal{A}$ is resilient on $(G, \mathcal{F}, \gamma, s, r)$, r must decide on the sender's message 0 in execution σ, and must do the same in execution σ'. However, in execution σ' the sender's message is 1. Therefore, $\mathcal{A}$ makes r decide on an incorrect message in $(G, \mathcal{F}', \gamma, s, r)$. This contradicts the assumption that $\mathcal{A}$ is safe. □

8.2.4 SUFFICIENCY OF CONDITION GRC

The *RMT Partial Knowledge Algorithm* (RMT-PKA) [74], presented below (Algorithm 8.19), is an RMT protocol which succeeds whenever the condition of Theorem 8.11 (in fact, its negation) is met, rendering it a tight condition on when RMT is possible. The following supplementary notions facilitate the proof.

In RMT-PKA there are two types of messages exchanged. *Type 1 messages* are used to propagate the sender's value and are of the form (x, p) where $x \in X$ and p is a path.[1] *Type 2 messages* of the form $((i, \gamma(i), \mathcal{F}_i), p)$ are used for every process i to propagate its initial information $\gamma(i), \mathcal{F}_i$ throughout the graph. Let M denote a subset of the messages of type 1 and 2 that the receiver process r receives at some round of the protocol on $(G, \mathcal{F}, \gamma, s, r)$. We will say that $value(M) = x$ if and only if all the type 1 messages of M report the same sender value x, i.e., for every such message (y, p), it holds that $y = x$, for some $x \in X$. Observe that M may consist of messages which contain contradictory information. Next, we determine the form of a message set M which contains no contradictory information in our setting (a valid set M).

Definition 8.12 Valid Set M. A set M of both type 1 and type 2 messages *corresponds to a valid scenario*, or more simply is *valid*, if

- $\exists x \in X$ s.t. $value(M) = x$. That is, all type 1 messages relay the same x as sender's value; and

- $\forall m_1, m_2 \in M$ of type 2, their first component (the part of the pair which comprises of the local information of a process) is the same when they refer to the same process. That is, if $m_1 = ((i, \gamma(i), \mathcal{F}_i), p)$ and $m_2 = (((j, \gamma'(j), \mathcal{F}_j'), p')$, then $i = j$ implies that $\gamma(i) = \gamma'(j)$ and $\mathcal{F}_i = \mathcal{F}_j'$.

---

[1]By $p\|i$ (appearing in the algorithm) we will denote the concatenation of path p with the id of process i. Also we use *tail*(p) to denote the last process of path p. Checking whether *tail*$(p) \neq j$, in line 6 of the algorithm, we ensure that at least one corrupted process will be included in a faulty propagation path.

Algorithm 8.19 RMT-PKA (RMT Partial Knowledge Algorithm)

(For process i)

Input of i: sender's label s, $\gamma(i)$, $\mathcal{F}_i$.

Additional input for $i = s$: value $x_s \in X$ (message space).

Type 1 message format: pair (x, p)

Type 2 message format: pair $((j, \gamma(j), \mathcal{F}_j), p)$,

where $x \in X$, j the id of some node, $\gamma(j)$ is the view of process j, $\mathcal{F}_j$ is the local adversary structure of process j, and p is a path of G (message's propagation trail).

```
 1: if i = s then                                              ▷ Code for s
 2:     send messages (x_s, {s}) and ((s, γ(s), F_s), {s}) to all neighbors and terminate.
 3: else if i ∉ {s, r}) then                                   ▷ Code for V \ {s, r}
 4:     send message ((i, γ(i), F_i), {i}) to all neighbors.
 5:     for any received type 1 or type 2 message (a, p) from process j do
 6:         if (i ∈ p) ∨ (tail(p) ≠ j) then
 7:             discard (a, p)
 8:         else
 9:             send (a, p||i) to all neighbors.
10:         end if
11:     end for
12: else if i = r then                                         ▷ Code for r
13:     Initialize M_r := ∅
14:     for any received type 1 or type 2 message (x, p) from process j do
15:         if (tail(p) ≠ j) then
16:             discard (x, p)
17:         else
18:             M_r := M_r ∪ (x, p)
19:         end if
20:         if (x, p) is a type 1 message then
21:             lastmsg := (x, p)
22:             if Decision(M_r, lastmsg) = x then
23:                 output x and terminate
24:             end if
25:         end if
26:     end for
27: end if
```

Algorithm 8.20 Decision(M_r, *lastmsg*)

1: **if** $r \in N_s$ **then**
2:     **if** *lastmsg* $= (x_s, \{s\})$ **then**
3:        **return** x_s
4:     **else**
5:        **return** $\bot$
6:     **end if**
7: **end if**
8: **for all** valid $M \subseteq M_r$ with *value*(M) = *value*(*lastmsg*) **do**
9:     compute graph G_M
10:     $M_1 := \{$type 1 messages of $M\}$
11:     $\mathcal{P}_1 := \{$ set of all paths p with $(x, p) \in M_1\}$
12:     $\mathcal{P}_{s,r} := \{$ set of all s-r paths of $G_M\}$
13:     **if** $(\mathcal{P}_{s,r} \subseteq \mathcal{P}_1) \wedge$ **Nocover**(M) **then**   ▷ *full message set with no*
14:        **return** *value*(*lastmsg*)   ▷ *adversary cover*
15:     **else**
16:        **return** $\bot$
17:     **end if**
18: **end for**

For every valid M we can define the pair (G_M, x_M) where $x_M = value(M)$; we assume that $x_M = \bot$ if no type 1 messages are included in M. To define G_M let V_M be the set of processes i for which the information $\gamma(i)$, $\mathcal{F}_i$ is included in M, namely $V_M = \{i \in V \mid ((i, \gamma(i), \mathcal{F}_i), p) \in M$ for some path $p\}$. Then, G_M is the node induced subgraph of graph $\gamma(V_M)$ on node set V_M. Therefore, a valid message set M uniquely determines the pair (G_M, x_M). We next propose two notions that we use to check if a valid set M contains correct information.

Definition 8.13 Full Message Set. A *full* message set M received by r is a valid set M, with *value*(M) $\neq \bot$, that contains all the s-r paths which appear in G_M as part of type 1 messages.

The definition of an *adversary cover* of a full message set M follows. Intuitively, if such a cut exists, then there is a scenario where all propagated values might be false.

Definition 8.14 Adversary Cover of Full Message Set M. A set $C \subseteq V_M$ is an *adversary cover* of full message set M if C has the following property: C is a cut between s and r on G_M and if B is the node set of the connected component that r lies in, it holds that $(C \cap V(\gamma(B))) \in \mathcal{F}_B$.

With the predicate $\texttt{nocover}(M)$ we will denote the non-existence of an adversary cover of M.

Algorithm 8.21 Nocover(M)

1: *check* ← **true**
2: **for all** $C \subseteq V_M$ **do**
3:     **if** C is a (s, r)-cut on G_M **then**
4:       $B :=$ the connected component of r in $G_M \setminus C$
5:       $(\mathcal{F}_B, V(\gamma(B))) := \bigoplus_{v \in B} (\mathcal{F}_v, V(\gamma(v)))$ ▷ *joint adversary structure*
6:       **if** $(C \cap V(\gamma(B))) \in \mathcal{F}_B$ **then**
7:         *check* :=**false**
8:       **end if**
9:     **end if**
10: **end for**
11: **return** *check*

The next theorem states the somewhat counterintuitive safety property of RMT-PKA, i.e., the receiver will never decide on an incorrect value despite the increased adversary's attack capabilities, which includes reporting fictitious nodes and false local knowledge. The proof can be found in [74].

Theorem 8.15   RMT-PKA Safety. *RMT-PKA is safe.*

The sufficiency proof combines techniques from [73] (correctness of the Path Propagation Agorithm) with the technical notions of full message set M, adversary cover of M and corresponding graph G_M, presented above and introduced in [74].

Theorem 8.16   Sufficiency. *Let $(G, \mathcal{F}, \gamma, s, r)$ be an RMT instance. If Condition GRC holds, then RMT-PKA achieves reliable message transmission in this instance.*

Proof. Observe that if $r \in N(s)$ then r trivially decides on x_s due to the *sender propagation rule*, since the sender is fault-free. Suppose that Condition GRC holds, i.e., that no RMT-cut exists; we will show that if $r \notin N(s)$ then r will decide on x_s due to the *full message set propagation rule*.

Let $T \in \mathcal{F}$ be any admissible corruption set and consider the run e_T of RMT-PKA where T is the actual corruption set. Let P be the set of all paths connecting s with r and are composed entirely by nodes in $V(G) \setminus T$ (fault-free nodes). Observe that $P \neq \emptyset$; otherwise T is a cut separating s from r which is trivially a RMT-cut, a contradiction.

Since paths in P are entirely composed by fault-free processes, it should be clear by the protocol that by round $|V(G)|$, r will have obtained x_s through all paths in P by receiving the corresponding type 1 messages M_1. Furthermore, by round $|V(G)|$, r will have received type 2 messages set M_2 which includes information for all the processes connected with r via paths that do not pass through nodes in T. This includes all nodes of paths in P. Consequently, r will have received the full message set $M = M_1 \cup M_2$ with $value(M) = x_s$.

We next show that there is no adversary cover for M and thus r will decide on x_s through the full message set propagation rule on M. Assume that there exists an adversary cover C for M. This, by definition means that C is a cut between s, r on G_M and if B is the node set of the connected component that r lies in, it holds that and $(C \cap V(\gamma(B))) \in \mathcal{F}_B$ (observe that r can compute $\mathcal{F}_B$ using the information contained in M_2 as defined in the previous paragraph). Then obviously $T \cup C$ is a cut in G separating s from r, since every path of G that connects s with r contains at least a node in $T \cup C$. Let the cut $T \cup C$ partition $V(G) \setminus \{T \cup C\}$ in the sets A, B s.t. $s \in A$. Then clearly $T \cup C$ is an RMT cut by definition, a contradiction. Thus, there is no adversary cover for M and r will decide on x_s. Moreover, since RMT-PKA is safe, the receiver will not decide on any other value different from x_s.   □

8.2.5   RELATION WITH CONSENSUS FEASIBILITY

In [40], the authors generalized the bound of $n > 3t$ for consensus feasibility in the case of a general adversary. Specifically, they show that consensus can be achieved if and only if there do not exist three sets $F_1, F_2, F_3 \in \mathcal{F}$ such that $F_1 \cup F_2 \cup F_3 \supseteq V$. The next corollary yields from the latter result, from the tightness of the non-existence of an RMT-cut for the feasibility of RMT and the fact that given an RMT sub-protocol, one can simulate any consensus solution for complete graphs. The proof is similar to that of Theorem 2.3.

Corollary 8.17   *For a graph $G = (V, E)$ and adversary structure $\mathcal{F}$, if there do not exist $F_1, F_2, F_3 \in \mathcal{F}$ with $F_1 \cup F_2 \cup F_3 \supseteq V$ and there does not exist an RMT-cut for any two processes $s, r \in V$, then exact consensus in a graph G under adversary structure $\mathcal{F}$ is possible.*

Observe that the condition is not necessary due to the fact that we consider only safe algorithms for RMT.

Bibliography

[1] Abraham, I., Amit, Y., and Dolev, D. Optimal resilience asynchronous approximate agreement. In *OPODIS*, pp. 229–239, 2004. DOI: 10.1007/11516798_17 14, 19, 23

[2] Alistarh, D., Gilbert, S., Guerraoui, R., and Travers, C. How to solve consensus in the smallest window of synchrony. In *Proc. of the 22nd International Symposium on Distributed Computing*, Berlin, Heidelberg, 2008. Springer-Verlag, pp. 32–46. DOI: 10.1007/978-3-540-87779-0_3 17

[3] Alistarh, D., Gilbert, S., Guerraoui, R., and Travers, C. Of choices, failures and asynchrony: The many faces of set agreement. *Algorithmica*, 62(1), pp. 595–629, 2012. DOI: 10.1007/s00453-011-9581-7 17

[4] Attiya, H. and Ellen, F. *Impossibility Results for Distributed Computing*. Morgan & Claypool, June 2014. DOI: 10.2200/s00551ed1v01y201311dct012 67

[5] Attiya, H., Lynch, N. A., and Shavit, N. Are wait-free algorithms fast? *Journal of the ACM*, 41(4), pp. 725–763, 1994. DOI: 10.1145/179812.179902 22, 23

[6] Attiya, H. and Welch, J. *Distributed Computing: Fundamentals, Simulations, and Advanced Topics*. Wiley Series on Parallel and Distributed Computing, 2004. 3, 5, 14, 15, 23, 45, 57

[7] Azadmanesh, M. H. and Kieckhafer, R. Asynchronous approximate agreement in partially connected networks. *International Journal of Parallel and Distributed Systems and Networks*, 5(1), pp. 26–34, 2002. 66

[8] Baldoni, R., Hélary, J., Raynal, M., and Tanguy, L. Consensus in Byzantine asynchronous systems. *Journal of Discrete Algorithms*, 1(2), pp. 185–210, 2003. DOI: 10.1016/s1570-8667(03)00025-x 16

[9] Bangalore, L., Choudhury, A., and Patra, A. Almost-surely terminating asynchronous Byzantine agreement revisited. In *Proc. of the ACM Symposium on Principles of Distributed Computing, (PODC)*, pp. 295–304, Egham, UK, July 23–27, 2018. DOI: 10.1145/3212734.3212735 16

[10] Bansal, P., Gopal, P., Gupta, A., Srinathan, K., and Vasishta, P. K. Byzantine agreement using partial authentication. In *Proc. of the 25th International Conference on Distributed*

Computing, pp. 389–403, Springer-Verlag, Berlin, Heidelberg, 2011. DOI: 10.1007/978-3-642-24100-0_38 15

[11] Benediktsson, J. A. and Swain, P. H. Consensus theoretic classification methods. *IEEE Transactions on Systems, Man, and Cybernetics*, 22(4), pp. 688–704, July 1992. DOI: 10.1109/21.156582 10

[12] Bertsekas, D. P. and Tsitsiklis, J. N. *Parallel and Distributed Computation: Numerical Methods*. Optimization and Neural Computation Series. Athena Scientific, 1997. 14, 15, 25, 37

[13] Biely, M., Robinson, P., and Schmid, U. Agreement in directed dynamic networks. In *Structural Information and Communication Complexity*, vol. 7355 of *Lecture Notes in Computer Science*. pp. 73–84, Springer Berlin Heidelberg, 2012. DOI: 10.1007/978-3-642-31104-8_7 37

[14] Biely, M., Robinson, P., Schmid, U., Schwarz, M., and Winkler, K. Gracefully degrading consensus and k-set agreement in directed dynamic networks. *CoRR abs/1408.0620*, 2014. DOI: 10.1007/978-3-319-26850-7_8 16

[15] Bonomi, S., Farina, G., and Tixeuil, S. Reliable broadcast in dynamic networks with locally bounded Byzantine failures. In *Stabilization, Safety, and Security of Distributed Systems—20th International Symposium, (SSS) Proceedings*, Tokyo, Japan, November 4–7, 2018, T. Izumi and P. Kuznetsov, Eds., vol. 11201 of *Lecture Notes in Computer Science*, pp. 170–185, Springer. DOI: 10.1007/978-3-030-03232-6_12 99

[16] Bouzid, Z., Mostfaoui, A., and Raynal, M. Minimal synchrony for Byzantine consensus. In *Proc. of the ACM Symposium on Principles of Distributed Computing, (PODC)*, pp. 461–470, New York, 2015. DOI: 10.1145/2767386.2767418 17

[17] Canetti, R. Universally composable security: A new paradigm for cryptographic protocols. In *42nd Annual Symposium on Foundations of Computer Science, FOCS*, pp. 136–145, IEEE Computer Society, Las Vegas, NV, October 14–17, 2001. DOI: 10.1109/sfcs.2001.959888 5

[18] Chandra, T. D., Hadzilacos, V., and Toueg, S. The weakest failure detector for solving consensus. *Journal of the ACM*, 43(4), pp. 685–722, 1996. DOI: 10.21236/ada253611 16

[19] Charron-Bost, B., Függer, M., and Nowak, T. Approximate consensus in highly dynamic networks. *CoRR abs/1408.0620*, 2014. DOI: 10.1007/978-3-662-47666-6_42 16, 37

[20] Charron-Bost, B., Függer, M., and Nowak, T. Approximate consensus in highly dynamic networks: The role of averaging algorithms. In *Automata, Languages, and Programming—42nd International Colloquium, (ICALP), Proceedings, Part II*, pp. 528–539, Kyoto, Japan, July 6–10, 2015. DOI: 10.1007/978-3-662-47666-6_42 19, 25

[21] Choudhury, A., Garimella, G., Patra, A., Ravi, D., and Sarkar, P. Crash-tolerant consensus in directed graph revisited (extended abstract). In *Structural Information and Communication Complexity—25th International Colloquium, (SIROCCO), Revised Selected Papers*, Ma'ale HaHamisha, Israel, June 18–21, 2018, Z. Lotker and B. Patt-Shamir, Eds., vol. 11085 of *Lecture Notes in Computer Science*, pp. 55–71, Springer. DOI: 10.1007/978-3-030-01325-7_10 42, 43

[22] Coan, B. A. Achieving consensus in fault-tolerant distributed computer systems: Protocols, lower bounds, and simulations. Ph.D. thesis, Cambridge, MA, 1987. 8

[23] Cybenko, G. Dynamic load balancing for distributed memory multiprocessors. *Journal of Parallel Distributed Computing*, 7(2), pp. 279–301, 1989. DOI: 10.1016/0743-7315(89)90021-x 10

[24] Dasgupta, S., Papadimitriou, C., and Vazirani, U. *Algorithms*. McGraw-Hill Higher Education, 2006. 59

[25] Dibaji, S. M., Ishii, H., and Tempo, R. Resilient randomized quantized consensus. *IEEE Transactions on Automatic Control*, 63(8), pp. 2508–2522, 2018. DOI: 10.1109/acc.2016.7526165 16

[26] Dolev, D. The Byzantine generals strike again. *Journal of Algorithms*, 3(1), March 1982. DOI: 10.1016/0196-6774(82)90004-9 15, 19, 95

[27] Dolev, D., Dwork, C., Waarts, O., and Yung, M. Perfectly secure message transmission. *Journal of the ACM*, 40(1), pp. 17–47, January 1993. DOI: 10.1109/fscs.1990.89522 19

[28] Dolev, D., Lynch, N. A., Pinter, S. S., Stark, E. W., and Weihl, W. E. Reaching approximate agreement in the presence of faults. *Journal of the ACM*, 33, pp. 499–516, May 1986. DOI: 10.21236/ada156541 10, 11, 12, 14, 19, 38, 39, 45, 54, 63, 65, 66, 83, 107

[29] Fekete, A. D. Asymptotically optimal algorithms for approximate agreement. In *Proc. of the 5th Annual ACM Symposium on Principles of Distributed Computing, (PODC)*, pp. 73–87, New York, 1986. DOI: 10.1007/bf01783662 19

[30] Fischer, M. J., Lynch, N. A., and Merritt, M. Easy impossibility proofs for distributed consensus problems. In *Proc. of the 4th Annual ACM Symposium on Principles of Distributed Computing, (PODC)*, pp. 59–70, New York, 1985. DOI: 10.1007/bfb0042333 14, 15, 16, 19, 22, 23, 67

[31] Fischer, M. J., Lynch, N. A., and Paterson, M. S. Impossibility of distributed consensus with one faulty process. *Journal of the ACM*, 32(2), pp. 374–382, April 1985. DOI: 10.1145/588059.588060 9, 22, 45

122 BIBLIOGRAPHY

[32] Fitzi, M. and Hirt, M. Optimally efficient multi-valued Byzantine agreement. In *Proc. of the 25th Annual ACM Symposium on Principles of Distributed Computing, (PODC)*, pp. 163–168, New York, 2006. DOI: 10.1145/1146381.1146407 17

[33] Friedman, R., Mostéfaoui, A., Rajsbaum, S., and Raynal, M. Distributed agreement and its relation with error-correcting codes. In *Distributed Computing, 16th International Conference, (DISC), Proceedings*, pp. 63–87, Toulouse, France, October 28–30, 2002. DOI: 10.1007/3-540-36108-1_5 16

[34] Függer, M. and Nowak, T. Fast multidimensional asymptotic and approximate consensus. In *32nd International Symposium on Distributed Computing, (DISC)*, New Orleans, LA, October 15–19, 2018. U. Schmid and J. Widder, Eds., vol. 121 of *LIPIcs*, pp. 27:1–27:16, Schloss Dagstuhl, Leibniz-Zentrum fuer Informatik. 16

[35] Függer, M., Nowak, T., and Schwarz, M. Tight bounds for asymptotic and approximate consensus. In *Proc. of the ACM Symposium on Principles of Distributed Computing, (PODC)*, pp. 325–334, Egham, UK, July 23–27, 2018. DOI: 10.1145/3212734.3212762 16

[36] Guerraoui, R., and Raynal, M. The information structure of indulgent consensus. *IEEE Transactions on Computers*, 53(4), pp. 453–466, 2004. DOI: 10.1109/tc.2004.1268403 16

[37] Halpern, J. Y. and Moses, Y. Knowledge and common knowledge in a distributed environment. *Journal of the ACM*, 37(3), pp. 549–587, July 1990. DOI: 10.1145/79147.79161 4

[38] Hamouma, M., Mostefaoui, A., and Trédan, G. *Byzantine Consensus with Few Synchronous Links*. Springer Berlin Heidelberg, Berlin, Heidelberg, 2007, chapter: Principles of Distributed Systems, *11th International Conference, (OPODIS), Proceedings*, pp. 76–89, Guadeloupe, French West Indies, December 17–20, 2007. DOI: 10.1007/978-3-540-77096-1_6 17

[39] Hegselmann, R. and Krause, U. Opinion dynamics and bounded confidence: Models, analysis and simulation. *Journal of Artificial Societies and Social Simulation*, 5, pp. 1–24, 2002. 10

[40] Hirt, M. and Maurer, U. M. Complete characterization of adversaries tolerable in secure multi-party computation (extended abstract). In *PODC*, pp. 25–34, J. E. Burns and H. Attiya, Eds., ACM, 1997. DOI: 10.1145/259380.259412 6, 15, 105, 106, 109, 117

[41] Ichimura, A. and Shigeno., M. A new parameter for a broadcast algorithm with locally bounded Byzantine faults. *Information Processing Letters*, June 2010. DOI: 10.1016/j.ipl.2010.04.003 92, 99

[42] Jadbabaie, A., Lin, J., and Morse, A. Coordination of groups of mobile autonomous agents using nearest neighbor rules. *Automatic Control, IEEE Transactions on*, 48(6), pp. 988–1001, June 2003. DOI: 10.1109/cdc.2002.1184304 14, 15, 25, 37

[43] Junqueira, F. and Marzullo, K. Synchronous consensus for dependent process failures. In *Distributed Computing Systems, Proceedings. 23rd International Conference on*, pp. 274–283, May 2003. DOI: 10.1109/icdcs.2003.1203476 106

[44] Kieckhafer, R. M. and Azadmanesh, M. H. Reaching approximate agreement with mixed-mode faults. *IEEE Transactions on Parallel and Distributed Systems*, 5(1), pp. 53–63, January 1994. DOI: 10.1109/71.262588 11, 12, 39, 45, 65, 107

[45] Koo, C.-Y. Broadcast in radio networks tolerating Byzantine adversarial behavior. In *Proc. of the 23rd Annual ACM Symposium on Principles of Distributed Computing, (PODC)*, pp. 275–282, New York, 2004, DOI: 10.1145/1011767.1011807 6, 91, 95, 96

[46] Kumar, M. V. N. A., Goundan, P. R., Srinathan, K., and Rangan, C. P. On perfectly secure communication over arbitrary networks. In *Proc. of the 21st Annual ACM Symposium on Principles of Distributed Computing, (PODC)*, A. Ricciardi, Ed., pp. 193–202, Monterey, CA, July 21–24, 2002. DOI: 10.1145/571855.571858 95

[47] Kuznetsov, P. Understanding non-uniform failure models. *Bulletin of the European Association for Theoretical Computer Science (BEATCS)*, 106, pp. 53–77, 2012. 106

[48] Lamport, L. The weak Byzantine generals problem. *Journal of the ACM*, 30(3), pp. 668–676, July 1983. DOI: 10.1145/2402.322398 9, 67

[49] Lamport, L. The part-time parliament. *ACM Transactions on Computer Systems*, 16(2), pp. 133–169, May 1998. DOI: 10.1145/279227.279229 14, 19

[50] Lamport, L., Shostak, R., and Pease, M. The Byzantine generals problem. *ACM Transactions on Programming Language Systems*, 4(3), pp. 382–401, July 1982. DOI: 10.1145/2402.322398 xvii, 6, 8, 15, 17, 21, 22, 91, 97

[51] LeBlanc, H. and Koutsoukos, X. Consensus in networked multi-agent systems with adversaries. *14th International Conference on Hybrid Systems: Computation and Control (HSCC)*, 2011. DOI: 10.1145/1967701.1967742 14, 19

[52] LeBlanc, H. and Koutsoukos, X. Low complexity resilient consensus in networked multi-agent systems with adversaries. *15th International Conference on Hybrid Systems: Computation and Control (HSCC)*, 2012. DOI: 10.1145/2185632.2185637

[53] LeBlanc, H., Zhang, H., Koutsoukos, X., and Sundaram, S. Resilient asymptotic consensus in robust networks. *IEEE Journal on Selected Areas in Communications: Special Issue on*

In-Network Computation, 31, pp. 766–781, April 2013. DOI: 10.1109/jsac.2013.130413 14, 15, 19, 38

[54] LeBlanc, H., Zhang, H., Sundaram, S., and Koutsoukos, X. Consensus of multi-agent networks in the presence of adversaries using only local information. *HiCoNs*, 2012. DOI: 10.1145/2185505.2185507 15, 107

[55] Liang, G. and Vaidya, N. Error-free multi-valued consensus with Byzantine failures. In *Proc. of the 30th Annual ACM SIGACT-SIGOPS Symposium on Principles of Distributed Computing, (PODC)*, pp. 11–20, New York, 2011. DOI: 10.21236/ada555083 17

[56] Litsas, C., Pagourtzis, A., and Sakavalas, D. A graph parameter that matches the re-silience of the certified propagation algorithm. In *Ad Hoc, Mobile, and Wireless Network— 12th International Conference, (ADHOC-NOW), Proceedings*, pp. 269–280, Wrocław, Poland, July 8–10, 2013. DOI: 10.1007/978-3-642-39247-4_23 92, 99, 100, 101, 102

[57] Lynch, N., Fischer, M., and Fowler, R. Simple and efficient Byzantine generals algo-rithm. In *Proc. of the Symposium on Reliability in Distributed Software and Database Systems*, pp. 46–52, IEEE, 1982. DOI: 10.21236/ada113241 17

[58] Lynch, N. A. *Distributed Algorithms*. Morgan Kaufmann, 1996. 3, 5, 11, 12, 14, 15, 21, 22, 23, 38, 39, 45, 57, 63, 65, 83, 84, 107

[59] Mendes, H. and Herlihy, M. Multidimensional approximate agreement in Byzantine asynchronous systems. In *STOC*, 2013. DOI: 10.1145/2488608.2488657 17

[60] Milosevic, Z., Hutle, M., and Schiper, A. Tolerating permanent and transient value faults. *Distributed Computing*, 27(1), pp. 55–77, 2014. DOI: 10.1007/s00446-013-0199-7 17

[61] Mostéfaoui, A., Moumen, H., and Raynal, M. Signature-free asynchronous binary Byzantine consensus with $t < n/3$, o(n2) messages, and O(1) expected time. *Journal of the ACM*, 62(4), pp. 31:1–31:21, 2015. DOI: 10.1145/2611462.2611468 16

[62] Mostéfaoui, A., Rajsbaum, S., and Raynal, M. Conditions on input vectors for consensus solvability in asynchronous distributed systems. *Journal of the ACM*, 50(6), pp. 922–954, 2003. DOI: 10.1145/380752.380792 16

[63] Mostéfaoui, A., Rajsbaum, S., Raynal, M., and Roy, M. A hierarchy of conditions for consensus solvability. In *Proc. of the 20th Annual ACM Symposium on Principles of Dis-tributed Computing, (PODC)*, pp. 151–160, Newport, RI, August 26–29, 2001. DOI: 10.1145/383962.384006 16

[64] Mostéfaoui, A., Rajsbaum, S., Raynal, M., and Roy, M. Condition-based protocols for set agreement problems. In *Distributed Computing, 16th International Conference, (DISC), Proceedings*, pp. 48–62, Toulouse, France, October 28–30, 2002. DOI: 10.1007/3-540-36108-1_4

[65] Mostéfaoui, A., Rajsbaum, S., Raynal, M., and Roy, M. Condition-based consensus solvability: A hierarchy of conditions and efficient protocols. *Distributed Computing*, 17(1), pp. 1–20, 2004. DOI: 10.1007/s00446-003-0093-9 16

[66] Mostéfaoui, A., Rajsbaum, S., Raynal, M., and Travers, C. The combined power of conditions and information on failures to solve asynchronous set agreement. *SIAM Journal of Computing*, 38(4), pp. 1574–1601, 2008. DOI: 10.1137/050645580 16

[67] Mostéfaoui, A. and Raynal, M. Solving consensus using Chandra–Toueg's unreliable failure detectors: A general quorum-based approach. In *Distributed Computing, 13th International Symposium, Proceedings*, pp. 49–63, Bratislava, Slovak Republic, September 27–29, 1999. DOI: 10.1007/3-540-48169-9_4 16

[68] Mostéfaoui, A. and Raynal, M. Leader-based consensus. *Parallel Processing Letters*, 11(1), pp. 95–107, 2001. 16

[69] Mostéfaoui, A. and Raynal, M. Signature-free asynchronous Byzantine systems: From multivalued to binary consensus with $t < n/3$, o(n2) messages, and constant time. In *Structural Information and Communication Complexity, 22nd International Colloquium, (SIROCCO) Post-Proceedings*, pp. 194–208, Montserrat, Spain, July 14–16, 2015. DOI: 10.1007/978-3-319-25258-2_14 17

[70] Mostéfaoui, A. and Raynal, M. Intrusion-tolerant broadcast and agreement abstractions in the presence of Byzantine processes. *IEEE Transactions on Parallel Distribution Systems*, 27(4), pp. 1085–1098, 2016. DOI: 10.1109/tpds.2015.2427797 17

[71] Mostéfaoui, A. and Raynal, M. Signature-free asynchronous Byzantine systems: From multivalued to binary consensus with $t < n/3$, O(n2) messages, and constant time. *Acta Informatica*, 2016. DOI: 10.1007/s00236-016-0269-y 17

[72] Neiger, G. Distributed consensus revisited. *Information Processing Letters*, 49(4), pp. 195–201, 1994. DOI: 10.1016/0020-0190(94)90011-6 9

[73] Pagourtzis, A., Panagiotakos, G., and Sakavalas, D. Reliable broadcast with respect to topology knowledge. *Distributed Computing*, 30(2), pp. 87–102, 2017. DOI: 10.1007/978-3-662-45174-8_8 14, 92, 94, 98, 99, 105, 109, 112, 116

[74] Pagourtzis, A., Panagiotakos, G., and Sakavalas, D. Reliable communication via semilattice properties of partial knowledge. In *Fundamentals of Computation Theory, 21st International Symposium, (FCT), Proceedings*, pp. 367–380, Bordeaux, France, September

11–13, 2017. DOI: 10.1007/978-3-662-55751-8_29 15, 105, 109, 110, 111, 112, 113, 116

[75] Patra, A. Error-free multi-valued broadcast and Byzantine agreement with optimal communication complexity. *Principles of Distributed Systems: 15th International Conference, (OPODIS), Proceedings*, pp. 34–49, Springer Berlin Heidelberg, Berlin, Heidelberg, Toulouse, France, December 13–16, 2011. DOI: 10.1007/978-3-642-25873-2_4 17

[76] Patra, A. and Rangan, C. P. Communication optimal multi-valued asynchronous broadcast protocol. *Progress in Cryptology—LATINCRYPT: 1st International Conference on Cryptology and Information Security in Latin America, Proceedings*, pp. 162–177, Springer Berlin Heidelberg, Berlin, Heidelberg, Puebla, Mexico, August 8–11, 2010. DOI: 10.1007/978-3-642-14712-8_10

[77] Patra, A. and Rangan, C. P. Communication optimal multi-valued asynchronous Byzantine agreement with optimal resilience. *Information Theoretic Security: 5th International Conference, (ICITS), Proceedings*, pp. 206–226, Springer Berlin Heidelberg, Berlin, Heidelberg, Amsterdam, The Netherlands, May 21–24, 2011. DOI: 10.1007/978-3-642-20728-0_19 17

[78] Pease, M., Shostak, R., and Lamport, L. Reaching agreement in the presence of faults. *Journal of the ACM*, 27(2), pp. 228–234, April 1980. DOI: 10.1145/322186.322188 xvii, 6, 14, 15, 17, 19, 21, 22

[79] Pelc, A. and Peleg., D. Broadcasting with locally bounded Byzantine faults. *Information Processing Letters*, 2005. DOI: 10.1016/j.ipl.2004.10.007 92, 93, 95, 97, 109, 110, 112

[80] Peleg, D. *Distributed Computing: A Locality-Sensitive Approach*. Society for Industrial and Applied Mathematics, 2000. DOI: 10.1137/1.9780898719772 3, 4, 5

[81] Raynal, M. *Distributed Algorithms for Message-Passing Systems*. Springer, 2013. DOI: 10.1007/978-3-642-38123-2 15

[82] Raynal, M. *Fault-Tolerant Message-Passing Distributed Systems—An Algorithmic Approach*. Springer, 2018. DOI: 10.1007/978-3-319-94141-7 15

[83] Raynal, M. and Stainer, J. Synchrony weakened by message adversaries vs. asynchrony restricted by failure detectors. In *ACM Symposium on Principles of Distributed Computing, (PODC)*, pp. 166–175, Montreal, QC, Canada, July 22–24, 2013. DOI: 10.1145/2484239.2484249 17

[84] Sakavalas, D., Tseng, L., and Vaidya, N. H. Effects of topology knowledge and relay depth on asynchronous consensus. *22nd International Conference on Principles of Distributed Systems, (OPODIS)*, Hong Kong, December 17–19, 2018. 14, 50, 77, 78, 80

[85] Sakavalas, D., Tseng, L., and Vaidya, N. H. Asynchronous crash-tolerant approximate consensus in directed graphs: Topology knowledge. *CoRR abs/1803.04513*, 2018. 50, 85

[86] Su, L. and Vaidya, N. Reaching approximate Byzantine consensus with multi-hop communication. In *Stabilization, Safety, and Security of Distributed Systems*, A. Pelc and A. A. Schwarzmann, Eds., vol. 9212 of *Lecture Notes in Computer Science*, pp. 21–35, Springer International Publishing, 2015. DOI: 10.1007/978-3-319-21741-3_2 14, 15, 19, 24, 25, 28, 30, 59, 77, 85, 86, 87

[87] Tseng, L. Fault-Tolerant Consensus in Directed Graphs and Convex Hull Consensus. Ph.D. thesis, University of Illinois at Urbana-Champaign, 2016. DOI: 10.1145/2767386.2767399 15, 28, 31, 59, 61, 66, 106

[88] Tseng, L. Recent results on fault-tolerant consensus in message-passing networks. In *Structural Information and Communication Complexity, 23rd International Colloquium, (SIROCCO), Revised Selected Papers*, pp. 92–108, Helsinki, Finland, July 19–21, 2016. DOI: 10.1007/978-3-319-48314-6_7 15

[89] Tseng, L., Vaidya, N., and Bhandari, V. Broadcast using certified propagation algorithm in presence of Byzantine faults. *Information Processing Letters*, 115(4), pp. 512–514, 2015. DOI: 10.21236/ada568117 14, 92, 99

[90] Tseng, L. and Vaidya, N. H. Exact Byzantine consensus in directed graphs. *CoRR abs/1208.5075*, 2012. DOI: 10.21236/ada568111 67, 68, 69, 73, 74, 75

[91] Tseng, L. and Vaidya, N. H. Asynchronous convex hull consensus in the presence of crash faults. In *Proc. of the ACM Symposium on Principles of Distributed Computing, (PODC)*, pp. 396–405, New York. DOI: 10.1145/2611462.2611470 17, 107

[92] Tseng, L. and Vaidya, N. H. Iterative approximate consensus in the presence of Byzantine link failures. In *Networked Systems, 2nd International Conference, (NETYS), Revised Selected Papers*, pp. 84–98, Marrakech, Morocco, May 15–17, 2014. DOI: 10.1007/978-3-319-09581-3_7 107

[93] Tseng, L. and Vaidya, N. H. Fault-tolerant consensus in directed graphs. In *Proc. of the ACM Symposium on Principles of Distributed Computing, (PODC)*, pp. 451–460, New York. DOI: 10.1145/2767386.2767399 15, 19, 24, 25, 28, 30, 37, 42, 53, 54, 59, 83, 84

[94] Tseng, L. and Vaidya, N. H. Iterative approximate Byzantine consensus under a generalized fault model. In *International Conference on Distributed Computing and Networking (ICDCN)*, January 2013. DOI: 10.21236/ada564090 15, 37, 105, 106, 107

[95] Turpin, R. and Coan, B. A. Extending binary Byzantine agreement to multivalued Byzantine agreement. In *Information Processing Letters*, 18, pp. 73–76, 1984. DOI: 10.1016/0020-0190(84)90027-9 17

[96] Vaidya, N. H. Iterative Byzantine vector consensus in incomplete graphs. In *International Conference on Distributed Computing and Networking (ICDCN)*, January 2014. DOI: 10.1007/978-3-642-45249-9_2 17

[97] Vaidya, N. H. and Garg, V. K. Byzantine vector consensus in complete graphs. In *Proc. of the ACM Symposium on Principles of Distributed Computing, (PODC)*, pp. 65–73, New York, 2013. DOI: 10.1145/2484239.2484256 17

[98] Vaidya, N. H., Tseng, L., and Liang, G. Iterative approximate Byzantine consensus in arbitrary directed graphs. In *Proc. of the 31st Annual ACM Symposium on Principles of Distributed Computing, (PODC)*, 2012. DOI: 10.1145/2332432.2332505 15, 19, 24, 25, 28, 30, 37, 59, 61, 64, 107

[99] Vicsek, T., Czirók, A., Ben-Jacob, E., Cohen, I., and Shochet, O. Novel type of phase transition in a system of self-driven particles. *Physical Review Letters*, 75, pp. 1226–1229, August 1995. DOI: 10.1103/physrevlett.75.1226 10

[100] West, D. B. *Introduction to Graph Theory*. Prentice Hall, 2001. 19, 21, 23, 24, 69

[101] Zhang, H. and Sundaram, S. Robustness of complex networks with implications for consensus and contagion. In *Proc. of CDC, the 51st IEEE Conference on Decision and Control*, 2012. DOI: 10.1109/cdc.2012.6425841 14, 15, 19

[102] Zhang, H. and Sundaram, S. Robustness of distributed algorithms to locally bounded adversaries. In *Proc. of ACC, the 31st American Control Conference*, 2012. 15

Authors' Biographies

DIMITRIS SAKAVALAS

Dimitris Sakavalas is currently a postdoctoral research fellow in the Computer Science department at Boston College. Previously, he has been a postdoctoral researcher at the Computation and Reasoning Laboratory of the National Technical University of Athens, Greece. He received his diploma (in Applied Mathematical and Physical Sciences), his M.Sc. (in Applied Mathematical Sciences), and his Ph.D. (in Computer Science) from the National Technical University of Athens, Greece, in 2009, 2012, and 2016, respectively. His research interests lie in the field of distributed computing, and range from complexity theory for distributed systems to fault-tolerant communication and agreement primitives as well as energy efficient wireless network protocols.

LEWIS TSENG

Lewis Tseng is currently an assistant professor in the Computer Science department at Boston College. Before that, he spent a year and a half as a researcher at Toyota InfoTechnology Center. He received a B.S. and a Ph.D. both in Computer Science from the University of Illinois at Urbana-Champaign (UIUC) in 2010 and 2016, respectively. His research broadly lies in the intersection of fault-tolerant computing and distributed computing. Some recent research includes: (i) fault-tolerant primitives, such as broadcast and consensus, in directed and incomplete networks; (ii) scalable distributed shared storage systems that tolerate crash and Byzantine faults; and (iii) fundamental understanding of Blockchain-based systems.

Printed in the United States
by Baker & Taylor Publisher Services